THE DAY

My Life Changed

D1690027

THE DAY My Life Changed

overcoming trauma to claim victory

TANYA C. STOKES

DREAM RELEASER
PUBLISHING

Copyright © 2022 by Tanya Stokes

Published by Dream Releaser Publishing

All rights reserved. No portion of this book may be reproduced, stored in a retrieval system, or transmitted in any form or by any means—electronic, mechanical, photocopy, recording, scanning, or other—except for brief quotations in critical reviews or articles, without prior written permission of the author.

Scripture quotations marked KJV are taken from the King James Version of the Bible. Public domain. Scripture quotations marked NIV are taken from the Holy Bible, New International Version®, NIV®. Copyright © 1973, 1978, 1984, 2011 by Biblica, Inc.™ Used by permission of Zondervan. All rights reserved worldwide. www.zondervan.com. The "NIV" and "New International Version" are trademarks registered in the United States Patent and Trademark Office by Biblica, Inc.™ | Scripture quotations marked NKJV are taken from the New King James Version®. Copyright © 1982 by Thomas Nelson. Used by permission. All rights reserved.

For foreign and subsidiary rights, contact the author.

Cover design by: Sara Young
Cover photo by: Silvia Jones (Inspirational Light Enterprise Photography)

ISBN: 978-1-959095-08-8   1 2 3 4 5 6 7 8 9 10

Printed in the United States of America

I dedicate this book to all those who would dare to rise from trauma.

CONTENTS

Acknowledgments ix

CHAPTER 1 *The Dream Team* 15

CHAPTER 2 *ER* 29

CHAPTER 3 *ICU* 41

CHAPTER 4 *I Am Not Alone* 55

CHAPTER 5 *The Journey to Recovery* 65

CHAPTER 6 *The Impact* 77

CHAPTER 7 *The Children's Perspectives* 87

CHAPTER 8 *Picking Up the Shattered Pieces* 103

CHAPTER 9 *I'm Hopeful* 115

CHAPTER 10 *The Final Say* 123

About the Author 133

Acknowledgments

To my Lord and Savior Jesus Christ, whom I serve with my whole heart.

To my husband of thirty-five years, Timothy: you have had the greatest impact on my life and destiny! I could not be who I am today without you. I love you forever.

To my four children, Brendon, Amber, Emmanuel, and Timothy II, who are the greatest joy of my life: you are all different yet significant. I couldn't imagine having lived without you. I love you forever.

To my late parents, Wiley C. Thomas and Georgianna Thomas: I have so much of both of you in me. You were amazing parents; I owe you the credit for who I have become.

To my late mother-in-love, Ethel Mary Stokes, who was like a mother when my mother passed: your support and encouragement always gave me the strength that I needed.

To my siblings, Emmogene Moore—who was the inspiration behind this work. I still remember the day you texted me to tell me you saw me writing a book called, *The Day My Life Changed*—Gail Freeman, Kimberley Hicks, Mary Hood, and Wiley C. Thomas Jr.: you're the best! We have all achieved great things in our own right. You have always stood by my side, built me up, and loved me. I stand on your shoulders.

x THE DAY *My Life Changed*

To my sisters-in-love, Sharon Stokes and Paula Hubbard: thank you for accepting me into the family and treating me as if I belonged.

To my church family: I am forever grateful for your love and loyalty. There are no words to truly express my gratitude. Without you, I would not have made it through the storms. Thank you.

To the senior leaders of Family Worship Center Church International—Min. Lisa Banks, Pastor Lenard Dotson, Min. Monique Dotson, Pastor James Hodo, Min. Dede Hodo, Prophetess Beverly Towns: you have literally lifted up my arms, have stood by me during my lowest moments, and have stepped up to the plate to help shoulder the ministry. I love you forever.

To the Family Worship Center Church International Ministry Staff—Min. Monique Dotson, Min. Dede Hodo, Pastor James Hodo, Min. Don McNeal, and Brandon Williams: you are a small team, but mighty in God. Your tireless service to the ministry is priceless. You have immeasurable worth in the mission of Family Worship Center Church International.

To Dr. Phillip Goudeaux: it is an honor to call you dad. You stretch me in ways beyond my comfort zone as you pull me higher into my purpose. Your words of affirmation, prayers, and continual encouragement have helped me to endure many trials.

To Dr. Brenda Goudeaux, my spiritual mother in whom lies the spirit of wisdom: you are a solid rock. I glean from your life whether I am up close or afar. You set a remarkable example of a woman after God's heart whom I emulate.

To Dr. David Ireland, my mentor and friend of our ministry: you have stood by our side for more than thirty years, offering priceless guidance that helped us navigate through many storms. You are a priceless treasure.

To Dr. Marlinda Ireland: thank you for the times that you lent me your ear, guided me with your wisdom, and for being a shoulder to cry on. I honor you for the example that you set as a Woman of Faith.

To Dr. Carolyn Driver: your entry into my life was divinely strategic. You have trained me as a coach, provided counsel that I believe saved my life, nurtured my potential, been a confidant, and through your presence in my life, I have been able to birth my dreams.

To Bishop Kirby Clements: I met you at one of the most strategic seasons of my life when I was literally at a crossroads. You cunningly guided me to make the right choice. Your insight and encouragement helped restore the self-confidence I needed to soar as the eagle that I know I am.

To Bishop T. D. Jakes: the fact that you keep standing strengthens me to stand. Your overcoming inspires me to overcome. You are an amazing gift to the body of Christ. Thank you for your sacrifice.

To Pastor Dan Rhodes: you have the true heart of a pastor. Thank you for lending me the needed guidance at the right time. I am forever grateful.

To Apostle Stephen Garner and Prophetess Yolanda Garner: you were a godsend. Thanks for coming alongside me to help strengthen the ministry. I appreciate your leadership, your love for us and the ministry, and how you continually check on us to make sure we are okay.

To Mother Ruth Pryor: you have set an example for all women of God, especially pastor wives. You serve tirelessly and with a heart of generosity. I am carrying a part of you in all that I do.

To Velma Johnson, Lynne Calloway, Priscilla Wallace, Karen Riptoe, LaTanga Christmas, and Cynthia Hoskins: you are my lifelong friends; some of our friendships span more than fifty years. You are rare treasures. We have had so many laughs together and even shared our heartbreaks, but the key is that we were together. You all know me well and it's been an absolute honor knowing you.

Special thanks to my friends Krystylle and Ben Richardson: you freely opened your home for my husband to get needed therapy and for me to rest. I am forever grateful for your love and generosity.

To Lady Carleen Holley, Prophetess Mary Johnson, Lady Andrea Richards, Pastor Alicia Frierson: thank you for standing by my side during the toughest moment of my life; you were there. Thanks for all the times of fellowship we have enjoyed, praying for and strengthening each other. Prophetess Mary Johnson, this book is a manifestation of things you spoke over my life during our fellowships. Thanks for obeying God.

To Marc and Bridgette Payne: I have always admired you as a power couple. You achieve great things together. Thank you for your generosity in allowing us to vacation at your home this summer. I was actually able to work on this book while relaxing and being refreshed.

To Leatrese Hopkins: you are a great workout partner; thank you for your listening ear as we walk and talk. I am able to bounce all my ideas (which seem endless) off of you and you actually want to hear them.

To Silvia Jones, photographer: thanks for always being available to help in the time of need. You are an amazing gift.

To Crystal Ashburn, makeup artist: you have a heart of gold. Thank you for responding whenever I need your help. I call you because you're the best.

To Andrea Richards, hair designer: thank you for caring enough to sacrifice your time to not only do my hair but to be present at the photoshoot to ensure things worked out. That's over-the-top service.

CHAPTER ONE

The Dream Team

OUR BEGINNINGS

We were "a match made in heaven," and everyone could tell we were a "perfect fit." Our strengths, values, passions, and dreams in life were in sync. One of my pastors told me, "You and Timothy have the highest level of agreement that I have ever seen in a couple." That was news to me because we weren't intentionally working on agreement; we just possessed it naturally as we were on the same path.

To be honest, our meeting was a fairytale. Our story began on the campus of Oakland University, his alma mater. I remember attending a gospel concert at Oakland University and they announced that they had Bible study on Monday evenings. I was eager to visit because the church I was attending at the time had midweek service too early for me to arrive on time after work. The very next day I went to the United Students for Christ Bible Study, not knowing it was a setup for a destiny moment. To be honest, I was just looking for God, not a husband. I was actually in a relationship already. But something

16 THE DAY *My Life Changed*

happened that was divine that night that changed the course of my life forever.

My would-be husband (who was a minister) announced that he was going to resume leadership of the Bible study (he had once led the group prior to graduating and returning home to Lansing, Michigan). His bags were still packed in his vehicle that night, being that it was his first day back on campus. He had returned to work in the Upward Bound Program, which focused on preparing underprivileged youth for college. I worked for Electronic Data Systems as a Chevrolet Customer Assistance Representative at the time.

In an attempt to connect with those in attendance, he passed around a sign-up sheet for our contact information. He had announced that he was doing a "Career Day" and wanted to invite some graduates as guests. Here's the kicker: He told me later, that when he approached me, there were words going off on the inside of him like a strobe light saying, "wife, wife, wife." He thought it was the devil. He had previously said he was done with his search for a wife.

To my surprise, I, too, was having an experience in my heart that was new to me. After I had written my name and number down, I privately spoke in my heart, *Lord, I hope he calls me,* although I wasn't in the market for a relationship. That shocked me because it was uncharacteristic. I see myself as a very loyal and faithful person. I accepted the invite to Career Day and the rest really is history. If it sounds like a fairy tale, it was and we were convinced that it was divine. We met February 9, 1987. I remember the date because it happens to be my father's birthday. Being convinced that it was the will of the

Lord, we were ready to pursue destiny together. We married September 26 of that same year.

As a young teenager, I vividly remember my mother making a statement in her anger: "All men are dogs." Although I was only a teenager at the time, I recall the prayer that I spoke in my heart to the Lord in response: *Lord, I know there is one out there for me.* Then I went outside to play sports because I was an athlete. There was one other simple request that I had of the Lord concerning a mate: *Lord, I just want a man of God.*

Never in my wildest imagination did I envision marrying a preacher. As I introduced him to my friends, they all confirmed that he was definitely the one for me. My dad told me years later that some of my family thought my husband's personality was too strong for me, so they were concerned. My dad, who knew me well, responded to their comments, "You don't have to worry about Tanya; she can handle herself." My childhood nickname was "Sweet Child." I am a kind person who loves people, but I have that side of me that won't allow myself to be run over. I think that's what my dad was reassuring my family of in his response to their concern. My prayer is that my family's story will encourage, strengthen, and inspire you to triumph in your storm.

WHO WAS TANYA?

I was born in Flint, Michigan, in April 1964, to hardworking parents. My father was an entrepreneur operating two businesses—real estate and his own personal income tax business. My mother was a schoolteacher. They both had risen from poverty to raise six children who were successful in their fields of interest ranging from a financial career to attorney to minister. Even in childhood, we were considered "the house on the block" where our friends and neighbors would gather. To me, we were a normal family who loved people. My parents were devoted to helping people who were in need. We didn't consider ourselves special per se, but once we were grown, our friends' perspectives confirmed that we were.

Athletics was an important part of my life growing up. I discovered my athletic skills at a young age, playing organized sports beginning in fourth grade. Sports brought great pleasure to my life. I probably played some form of sports nearly every day, except Sunday, due to my faithful attendance at church. Besides athletics, I also excelled as class president for four years, performed in the marching band, was a member of the Honor Society, and participated in oratorical competition at my church. One of my highest achievements, besides being on a championship basketball team, was being named Flint's Female Athlete of the Year in 1982. I was also inducted into two local athletic halls of fame: the Genesee Regional Hall of Fame in 2002 and the Greater Flint African American Sports Hall of Fame as a member of the Lady Vikings basketball team in 2019. I was also individually inducted into the Greater Flint African American Sports Hall of Fame in 2009.

I earned a degree in broadcasting and cinematic arts at Central Michigan University in 1986, with a double major in broadcasting and journalism. My dream was to become a television news anchor. I later earned my Master's degree in Theology from Moody Theological Seminary in May 2015.

WHO WAS TIMOTHY?

My husband was born on August 18, 1960, in Lansing, Michigan. He is the only son of Paul and Ethel Stokes. His two siblings—an older and younger sister—rightfully accused their mom of my husband being her favorite. She never confirmed this, but it was obvious that he was her pride and joy. His relationship with his father was pretty rocky. He described his dad as "mean," even to the point of being afraid of him. That lack of relationship ended up being a source of rejection and deep emotional pain. My husband was strong in academics and loved to be the life of the party. At an early age, he often spoke of his desire to be a public speaker. He never forgot the life-changing moment when his cousin informed him, "You have to have something to say." That was his first time ever considering the message. He would often brag about playing on the same basketball court that the famed basketball player Ervin (Magic) Johnson played on (because they lived in the same neighborhood).

When we met, he was a very bold, outgoing, visionary type of guy who found his passion in helping others discover their potential. He had keen perception in identifying gifts in people; even if they couldn't see it, his eagle eyes would pick it up. Thus, he habitually identified the gift within a person and helped them to see and develop it as the gift was nurtured through training. Then he would give the person a platform to utilize his or her gift. He's an amazing person, who could be described as a "pioneering visionary, focused, charismatic, driven, creative, and even ahead of his time." These are words that I've often heard concerning him. When you meet him, it's obvious that you have never met anyone like him. Along with that, he is very humorous when he relaxes from being so serious. He earned two degrees from Oakland University in Rochester, Michigan: one in business and the other in communications. He was also scheduled to graduate with me in May of 2015 from Moody Theological Seminary with a Master's degree in Theology.

WHO WE WERE TOGETHER

We call each other "sweetheart." Looking at our lives from the outside would have been "enviable," as I have heard people describe us. One woman even spoke of me as being a woman "who had everything." Although this wasn't my personal perspective of my life, marriage, and family, in retrospect, I can see why some held that view. We were what people have called "a power couple—TNT" (standing for Timothy and Tanya), a young couple full of passionate purpose to help people, devoted to God, educated, family-oriented, successful at whatever we set out to achieve together, and living our dreams to do a great work for the Lord.

I would often say, "If my husband could dream it, I could birth it." We had just the right mixture of strengths, as well as like-mindedness, to achieve what we envisioned or believed was the will of the Lord for our lives. This pursuit of godly purpose eventually led us back to my hometown of Flint to found a ministry (Family Worship Center Church International) on September 4, 1991. We were young, strong, and full of hope that we could impact the lives of many by empowering them to live for Christ. The ministry was successful. Under our leadership, it grew to become one of the largest ministries in our region, located off a major highway on 137 acres. We were able to build the 35,000-square-foot facility (with 1,000-seat auditorium) that houses the ministry. Building anything successful comes with a tremendous price that others can't fully see or comprehend unless you live it firsthand.

> *Building anything successful comes with a tremendous price that others can't fully see or comprehend unless you live it firsthand.*

Over time, I realized that we worked so well together and had so much work on our plates with a growing ministry and family that it began to feel like we were business partners. Our time together was spent handling all the matters at hand, whether it was church or family related with the busy schedules of four children. When I realized what was occurring, I tried diligently to find the "balance." I believe that's the challenge of every pastor and ministry family because there are demands literally 24/7. We didn't have anyone guiding us through the trials of building a successful ministry and maintaining the proper boundaries between church life and home life. As with everything we had done, we attempted to pioneer and navigate our way through it with the wisdom and knowledge we acquired along the way.

At some point, the demands took their toll on our lives. Sometimes you can give so much to where you prioritize others to the neglect of yourself. We both fell into that trap over time. When do you get an opportunity to stop? How do you really refresh? Who ministers to the minister? That's the question.

THE FUTURE WAS BRIGHT

Neither of us (my husband nor I) knew how to do things with half effort. We operate with an "in it to win it" type mentality, running hard, giving it 100-percent effort. We strongly believe in leaving it all on the court. We were definitely soul mates envisioning the same goals, same values, and same philosophy of living. It was that kind of "agreement" that the strength of our union was founded upon. We were pioneers, charting a path that hadn't been trodden—bringing unique strategies to lift people's lives to the next level.

My husband was known for his profound teaching that was transformational. We have a motto at the church that it's "a place where you can grow," an idea that was born from my husband's life purpose to "discover, develop and deploy" potential—he was thriving in his gift. Many were attracted to the life-changing word he preached. We have many other facets of the ministry that were vital to its growth: the worship, training, prayer ministry, a great ministry team, and the family culture that we were able to establish. We only had plans to continue expanding when calamity struck. During the economic downturn of 2009, shortly after we had moved into the new facility, the credit union (that was getting rid of their church contracts nationwide) foreclosed on the property. By a miracle of God, we were able to repurchase it with a discount of three million dollars! That was one of many battles we experienced. It seemed as if we had experienced enough trials already when the unimaginable occurred.

THE UNIMAGINABLE

I will never forget Friday, March 13, 2015. It was the day that my life changed forever. I vividly remember the day prior, the thought crossing my mind, *Tomorrow is Friday the 13th, but it has always been an uneventful day for me.* Although many people are superstitious of that day, I'm not. Ironically, that ended up being the day that my life changed.

I will never forget Friday, March 13, 2015. It was the day that my life changed forever.

It was a normal day; my husband had gotten back on his workout regimen, rejoining me at the gym two weeks prior. I was glad that he had accompanied me and was getting back on track. We worked out three times a week. He doesn't know how to ease back into a workout because he does everything with one level of intensity—"strongly." So, he was lifting weights as if he hadn't taken a break. Even that day, he had pushed himself hard, perhaps competing with the men in the training group. As a former athlete, I understand the mindset; I don't want to be the weakest link in the group either. Anyhow, we left the gym and shared just a few words, which would end up being our last conversation. We live about five minutes from the gym, but on the drive home, he spoke of how he would be back in shape in about a couple weeks. I just listened, although I thought it was quite a "lofty" goal and I knew that it was going to take a lot longer, but I've learned that I don't have to express all my thoughts, so I just kept quiet.

We arrived home in time for him to jump in the shower and head out to the movies with our only daughter, Amber. She was on Spring Break from college and he wanted to take her on a date. They were at the movies and I took advantage of having time alone to finish my final paper to earn my master's degree. I was pressing toward the finish line, as graduation was in May, and I was focused on finishing the four-year program that had turned into a long seventeen-year journey to the finish line.

I texted him and told him to drop Amber off at work (which was a thirty-minute drive), being that the movie would end close to her work time. I heard him arrive home after dropping her off at work. With plans to videotape one of our new member's class teachings, I thought he lingered downstairs to have our son Emmanuel begin the taping. After not hearing him, I went downstairs to see where he was. I didn't see him, so I circled back upstairs and went back into the bedroom to resume writing. Shortly thereafter, he entered the room in his shorts that he normally relaxed in and made a beeline to the bed. In retrospect, I don't think he even saw me sitting there.

It was weird because for some reason, I didn't say anything either, perhaps because I knew he was heading to bed.

It was unusual for him to take a nap, but I had probably nagged my husband for several years by that time for not getting the proper amount of rest. As his "suitable helper," I would chime in when I felt he was out of balance. He insisted that he didn't require a lot of rest saying, that if he went to bed around 9:00 p.m., he would wake up in the wee hours of the morning. I do agree that he didn't require the full eight hours that I did, but I still couldn't understand how he could function on the little sleep I observed. So that day, it was natural for me to conclude that he was taking a nap because "sleep had finally caught up with him." It wasn't until sometime later into this journey that I discovered he had kept indicating that he was tired when he was at the movie with our daughter.

He was sleeping hard though, and since I was always in bed first, I really didn't hear his sleep tones. As I typed my paper, I would glance over at him every now and then because I was very aware of his presence. At one point, he raised his left arm in the air, opened and closed his fist, and then went back to sleep. When I witnessed that, my conclusion was maybe his hand had fallen asleep, like mine does at times, and I open and close my fist in the same way to get the circulation flowing. In hindsight, it was at this time that he was probably having the stroke. One other time, he tried to move by slightly lifting up his right shoulder as if he were going to sit up but laid back down again, falling asleep. I even lay down (although I couldn't fall asleep) for about thirty minutes next to him before I left at four thirty to pick my daughter up from work. We arrived home at approximately 5:35 p.m., and I remember telling her in the car that her dad had made a couple "strange moves" in his sleep.

Upon entering the house, I went to the kitchen to start dinner. My daughter was there with me and insisted that I go upstairs and finish my paper. She was determined to cook alone. I didn't really want the burden on her to cook both meals that day (because of her dad being vegetarian, we always had to cook separate meals). I decided to take her up on her offer being that my paper awaited me, so I went immediately upstairs to resume my work.

Upon opening the bedroom door, I noticed that the comforter was slightly off my husband, but I didn't get a good look because I passed by the end of the bed headed to my chaise lounge across the room. That is when it hit me to inquire if he was okay because he had been in bed so long. I sat down, looking towards his side of the bed (which was the far side of the room), and I asked, "Sweetheart, are you alright?" As soon as I got the words out of my mouth, he began to throw up.

At this point, everything was coming together for me that he didn't feel well. But when I saw the look in his eyes as he threw up, it wasn't a normal look when you just have a stomachache. He was flat on his back, not lifting up at all. I can't even describe his eyes; it was, I'm sure, a look of death as he lay there helplessly. I ran to the banister to yell downstairs to my daughter to have her call Beverly Towns (the woman in our ministry who heads up the prayer ministry) to have her pray as I called 911 to let them know my husband was sick. When I threw the comforter off of him, I realized he had wet the bed, so he couldn't get up (it also explained why he didn't sit up while vomiting). At the same time, I grabbed a towel to remove the vomit so he wouldn't choke. This all happened in a matter of seconds because I was moving quickly as my mind was putting all the pieces of the puzzle together. I had never dealt with anything like this, but I knew it was serious even though I was still clueless as to the nature of his illness.

My guess would be the ambulance was there within five minutes, being that we live near the hospital. I hadn't even gotten his shirt off from the vomit. We changed his shirt as the paramedic said, "It looks like a stroke," and put him on the stretcher and quickly headed to the hospital. I went in my closet to change clothes when my daughter entered my room. This was a moment I will never forget. As she looked at me, she said, "Mom, we got this! We're champions, right?" and I looked at her and responded, "Yes, we're champions." That was a moment etched in my memory forever. Being a champion is something I engrained in my children from my life experience as a champion athlete. That's my approach to everything I do in life, even parenting. She was nineteen at the time. My eldest son Brendon and youngest son Timothy had arrived home from school. Timothy was a 13-year-old ninth grader and Brendon was a 22-year-old college senior. By the time of the stroke, Emmanuel (our 18-year-old middle son) had left to attend a basketball game at his former high school.

On my way to the hospital, I had the presence of mind to call my mother-in-law to inform her of the situation. She had a very sober tone and said she would be down in the morning. She lives around fifty minutes from us. I called our associate pastor and two others on the senior leadership team, and I texted my sister while in the emergency room to notify my family. That was all I could do now that the fight for his life was in motion.

CHAPTER TWO
ER

WHAT HAPPENED?

The question (if I could have formed it into words) while I was watching my husband fight for his life in the ER was, "How did we get here?"

Were the signs glaring, but I was too close to see them? Were we just overly confident that "this would never happen to him" because of his health history? I had probably only seen him sick with a cold a couple times in twenty-seven years of marriage. We thought he had taken the necessary dietary precautions that would avert him from having a heart attack like the one that had taken the life of his dad. He had become a vegetarian thirty-four years earlier as a college student and had exercised through the years, although not as consistently as he could have.

The stress of his position as lead pastor was evident. I even felt the tremendous weight of ministry as I worked alongside him. It's hard to describe or even put in words the burden that you feel when you are a public servant. It's like a 24/7 job which you can't escape. The only true escape time is when you're asleep (in my experience) because nearly every waking hour presents an opportunity for you to think about some aspect of your responsibility. You may find yourself pondering the solution to an unsolved problem, mentally carrying the burden of raising the funds needed to support the work, the struggle to get enough people to help shoulder the vision, or the complexities that people face in their lives in which you desire to counsel or help bring solutions.

There's also the demand for leadership and guidance of the vision that taxes you mentally, emotionally, and physically, not to mention the hours of study and prayer time to have something to give the people. The wife, the children, the extended family—oh, I almost forgot—then yourself. That may not be the exact order, but that's my perspective from my years of experience. I found that being the one who worked hard to build a stable family in the midst of unimaginable demands on our life, I most certainly was last in my own life, so I'm pretty confident that he was too. People see the glory and the successful results of your labor, but they don't see the price.

All success comes with a price tag attached. All leaders will verify that this is true. At a time like this, one can't help but ask, "Was it worth it?" This is all hindsight as I write, although it's a legitimate question to consider, and I am sharing it now to perhaps inspire people who can be labeled "workaholics" or those who simply struggle to find balance in their lives and family. As a spouse, your mate is that balance; he or she will know when things are off course. Listening to the voice of your spouse is critically important. Another person observing you can help you see things that may be in your blind spots.

THE ER EXPERIENCE

It was a stroke, confirming the initial findings of the medical staff who arrived at our home. It seemed like forever as I eagerly waited for the medical staff to perform all of their procedures to obtain a diagnosis. The initial CAT scan didn't show any bleeding on the brain, so I was somewhat relieved. It seemed like hours later when they took another CAT scan on his neck and found that he had a massive stroke on the left side of the brain, which affected movement on the right side and the speech center. They didn't explain all of that to me at the time. Of course, that was troubling news, but I still didn't know the impact on the life level. It was a couple of months before I understood the ramifications.

The ER was where my mind was in a fog, almost disbelief that I was there and my husband was lying on the table in front of me. To make matters worse, a male nurse came in to attend to him and said, "Sir, you are a very sick man." I couldn't believe my ears. I just wasn't used to a nurse telling a patient his condition and definitely not speaking so bluntly. I still didn't know what that really meant or the severity of his medical condition.

The medical staff asked me a lot of questions and concluded that they wouldn't be able to administer a medicine to help break up the effects of the stroke because of the time lapse. If administered after a three-hour period, it could kill the patient, so that was not an option. To my recollection, it had been more than three hours from the time I estimated that he had taken the nap and the time they had done their preliminary analysis. After the MRI results, they immediately put him on life support, explaining that it was a part of the normal procedure.

When our middle son Emmanuel arrived, another moment occurred. The kids stood by my husband's side, but at a slight distance. My husband had the presence of mind to extend his arm to reach out for them, beckoning them to draw near to assure them that he would be okay. They grabbed his hand; no words were spoken. We all just stared in bewilderment. They spent a lot of their time in the lobby with the church leaders and others who had assembled in the waiting room. I was told later that they prayed and cried together. I didn't know who was there or how people had heard about what was going on. I remained in the ER by his side, limiting the visits because my focus was solely on my husband and the fight for his life. I sat by his side and prayed. That's all I knew to do.

It was the ER, so he wasn't the only patient in the room, although the curtains were drawn for privacy. As I sat there alone at one point during the night, I heard the nurses working on someone. I ascertained that they were working to save the person's life. I said a prayer for whoever it was. I heard the heart monitoring machine go flat, like in the movies, and I realized the person didn't make it and the medical personnel's comment, in disappointment, "I tried really hard to save him," confirmed that reality. I later found out that it was a 17-year-old young man who was involved in a horrific car accident. I was saddened by that, even in my own trauma that I was experiencing in the ER.

THE FIGHT FOR HIS LIFE

I never imagined being behind the scenes in a medical emergency and hearing the staff work to save someone's life. I saw how much they really care about people and are invested in doing whatever they can to save a life. That's amazing, while at the same time extremely sobering when their attempt fails. I felt all of that as I sat by my husband, who was also fighting for his life.

I remember my sister coming in and sitting next to me, for which I'm truly grateful—to have a wonderful, supportive family. She started to cry as she spoke of my husband, and I couldn't handle it. I (hopefully lovingly) asked her not to cry. You would have to understand my personality to not be stunned or offended by that statement. In my world, I had assessed that I needed someone to pray, not cry—we had to fight.

Fighting was just the zone that I was in, having been a cancer survivor at the age of twenty-eight. I, too, was fully acquainted with the fight to survive. The uterine cancer that I had from an irregular pregnancy was so aggressive that it required the maximum dosage of chemotherapy in an attempt to save my life. I received weekly treatments, with every other week being an all-night stay in the hospital to receive twelve hours of chemotherapy. I was labeled a "high-risk" patient.

During my very first stay in the hospital for treatment, there was a death a couple doors down from my room. This resulted in a lot of commotion in the hallway from a family who was deeply grieving. Our former pastor had gone down to console them and overheard my doctor tell them to quiet down because "There's a young lady who is down the hallway fighting for her life." Of course, he didn't reveal that to us that day. We knew it was a serious condition in my body, but things were moving so quickly that we hadn't had time to process its severity.

Once my doctor knew that I needed additional medical attention, she called Timothy and me on a Thursday evening to explain. I had a meeting with the oncologist on Monday, and after his evaluation, he checked me into the hospital the following day because of how aggressive the cancer was in my body. He explained that the cancer had already protruded through the walls of my uterus. While hospitalized, I would take my Bible and books to read and rarely have guests other than Timothy. Our firstborn was only six months at the time. I felt that I just needed to cling to God, which is exactly how I felt in that ER while we battled for Timothy's life. His medical condition was very different, but in many ways the feelings were the same, and both were life or death.

Before I knew it, it was 9:00 a.m. the next day. I had sat in the ER by his bedside all night. I was told the neurologist was going to come in and speak with me. She arrived and set up a private meeting to discuss her assessment and recommendation. After she explained everything, I had to bring in my niece (who is a nurse), my sister, and a couple ministry leaders who were there so they, too, could hear what she was recommending, so I could make the right decision.

The neurologist said, "The damage has been done. I want to do surgery to remove the skull cap because the brain is going to swell from the injury and the fluid needs some place to go. You can choose to do nothing like some people choose, but if you do nothing, there could be more damage." At the time, I still couldn't process what the "damage" was that she was referring to, but I knew I wanted to prevent further damage, even though I didn't want to remove his skull cap. It would require major surgery that evening, and she would put the skull cap in his belly until it was time to put it back on, which would require another major surgery. I wanted desperately to do what was best for him (and only what I deemed necessary) to give him the best chance to recover. We all felt surgery was the best option; then came the meltdown. One of the ministers prayed while we all cried and held each other.

I agreed to the surgery. It was around 11:30 a.m.; they ended up taking him in around 4:00 p.m. to prep him for his 5:00 p.m. surgery. One pastor—who considered my husband to be *his* pastor—and his wife traveled all the way from Gary, Indiana, to be there. By that time, I realized I had been up about a day and a half straight. I tried to lie down on a sofa while he was in surgery but couldn't really rest. I knew it was major surgery and was eager to see him on the other side. By then, several people were gathered in the waiting room with us in support; we occupied pretty much the entire area. It seemed like forever, but he finally came out of surgery around 10:00 p.m. The surgery was a success, and I watched them immediately wheel him to ICU.

MY MENTAL AND EMOTIONAL STATES

If I could have interpreted my feelings, my discussion with God would have gone like this: "I don't get it, God, but I know You have been my God all my life. I gave my heart to You when I was twelve years old. The one prayer I remember from my youth as I knelt beside my bed was, 'Lord, I will do whatever You want me to do.' Lord, I don't understand; I don't have the wherewithal to wrap my mind around this trauma, let alone process how we got here and what the future holds."

The only things that gave me temporary emotional relief were the prayers of the saints, the support of those who were present in the storm, and my history with God. During our stay in the ICU waiting room, we experienced a few moments of joy. One was when my youngest son, Timothy II, was telling some jokes to me and two of my best friends from my elementary school days who were by my side. For some reason, we laughed at all of his jokes to the point of crying (as I do when I get really tickled). It was moments like those that took my mind away from the new reality that I was living.

I really couldn't think about anything else but what it would take for my husband to survive this major trauma, with the hopes of him fully recovering and returning to ministry. I envisioned being able to present him back to the church (who loved him dearly), healed and ready to lead us into the next phase of ministry. I wanted my family to be together again as we once were described—"a close-knit family."

I really couldn't think about anything else but what it would take for my husband to survive this major trauma, with the hopes of him fully recovering and returning to ministry.

I managed to call two people, our spiritual father and a mentor who was a longtime friend of the ministry, to inform them of the tragedy and to receive much-needed counsel as to how I should proceed. Thankfully, we also had church members who had been a part of the ministry since its inception (nearly twenty-four years prior at that time). Many of the leaders also had that level of longevity and "skin in the game," and they weren't going to leave us then. They stepped up to the plate and provided the leadership necessary to continue in our absence. I'm forever grateful for them and the church family, those who remained, who banded together in support of us and the ministry.

The word got out quickly, with him being a popular public figure and living in a small gossipy town where people are very much interested in the latest news, especially in church circles. People were texting me from all over the country: those who were former members who had relocated in years prior, pastors and other leaders, friends, and family. It was exhausting to try to explain the situation over and over again. I began to tell people we would post an update on our ministry website because I needed to continue to focus on winning the battle.

I think one of the hardest things to see is the scope of your impact while you are living. With the overwhelming outpouring of prayers and concern, it was profound to me that I was experiencing a glimpse of the significance of his life. I was encouraged in knowing how far-reaching his life and ministry had been.

LIFE IN THE TRENCHES

As with war, there is only one thought: *We need to get out of this alive to return back to our families*. In the movie *Top Gun: Maverick*, Tom Cruise led a group of fighter pilots on an impossible mission. His superiors seemed to be okay with the sacrifice of life that would possibly occur during this mission. His superiors' perspective was that the pilots were fully aware of the risk or possibility of losing their lives. But Cruise's mission was for them to return back to their families. That was my mission too. I had a single focus on my husband not only surviving this tragedy but fully recovering from its devastation.

There's a poem called "Footprints in the Sand" that begins with a person walking in the sand with God alongside him. At a particular point on the journey (which was the saddest and most troublesome time in his life), he noticed that there was only one set of footprints in the sand. Bewildered by this, he asked God why there was only one set of footprints at that point of the journey in which he needed Him the most. God's response was, "During your trials and testings, when you saw only one set of footprints, it was then that I carried you."

If I were to reflect on the question, "How did I survive the battle mentally, emotionally, physically, and spiritually?" I would definitely respond, "It was the Lord by my side." In my experience, trauma is the time when new depths of relationship with Jesus Christ are forged, as when I had to fight for my own life with cancer. In my mind, there is no other help that I know. Of course, it's always good and comforting to have people by your side, but nobody can fully understand the depths of your pain unless they are truly in your shoes. I didn't even have time to process the impact of this horrific life-or-death experience because we were in the heat of the battle.

THE NEW NORM

Life as we had previously known it was gone forever. Change was imposed upon us, whether we invited it or not or liked it or not; change happened. I would call it total devastation, a catastrophic loss. I hadn't even processed it as loss while in the trenches because I didn't know what the future would hold, and my hopes were still alive that something good would come of it. Literally living at the hospital was the norm for me. All of the children were still living at home at the time; one was in middle school, and the others were attending college locally. I don't even know how they survived while I was at the hospital. They would visit, but they had to go on with their lives as well. Although this trauma drastically impacted our family, I was determined to carry the brunt of it on my shoulders. I guess I was attempting to protect what little normalcy they had left, so I desired them to continue to pursue their education and find their life's path.

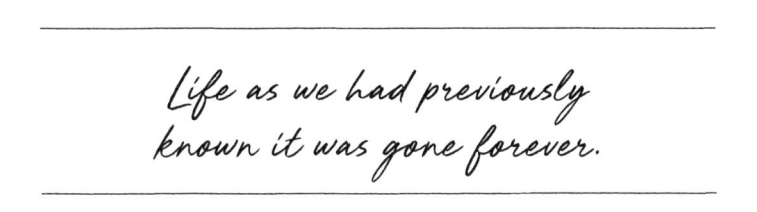

Life as we had previously known it was gone forever.

This was just the beginning of a very long journey to try to recover what we had lost. I remember around day seven, going home to sleep in my own bed for a couple hours' nap. Oh, the memories were flooding my mind as I recalled the day my life changed. His side of the bed was empty. Home felt strangely different. Our entire world had shifted. It appeared that life outside of the hospital had kept progressing while we, who had once been a thriving family, just struggled to survive one day at a time.

CHAPTER THREE
ICV

WILL HE SURVIVE?

This next part of our journey took place in ICU room 525, where Timothy would spend eleven days before being released to rehab. I began to chronicle his journey while the details were still fresh in my mind. He arrived in ICU immediately following his surgery, so it was after 10 p.m. on day two. I was still up since the morning of the stroke, Friday the 13th. Although the surgery was successful, I learned that he still was not out of danger. His blood pressure had dropped after surgery, so they gave him medicine to raise it. However, they couldn't get it to stabilize; that was an extremely rough night for both of us. His blood pressure was around 243/103. I pretty much stayed up all night to monitor his blood pressure because I couldn't rest knowing it was critically high.

While he was in surgery, I had to meet with our church's senior leadership team to discuss how we would proceed with the ministry. They drafted a letter to be posted on our website to inform people of what happened and that they could receive updates there as we had additional news. We discussed all the details of how the announcement would be made.

Back in the waiting room were a few family members and friends who pretty much had set up camp with blankets, pillows, food, and drink that people graciously had brought us. That night, my sister Gail, my niece Akilah, and her son KeShaun stayed overnight with me.

THE FIRST BREAKTHROUGH

Day three was Sunday morning, which had arrived quickly. After not sleeping too well in the waiting room chairs, I woke up to prepare to watch our church service live stream. A hospital representative pulled me to the side that day to inform me that we couldn't occupy the entire waiting room, but that was the least of my concerns. All I knew was that I wasn't leaving. I stayed by his side the entire eleven days.

I was informed that church was packed that day; of course, it was because of the rumors traveling throughout the city since Friday. As expected, the people were crushed, totally heartbroken about their beloved pastor's condition. Of course, they were wondering if he would survive or recover. Church service ended at noon. At the hospital, it was 1:00 p.m. when they finally stabilized him. But I felt that we were over the hump, so to speak. I didn't know that this was just the beginning of that leg of the journey.

I entertained a lot of guests all day. Being that they stabilized him, that was a breakthrough moment for me. I was then able to laugh and joke with friends and family for the rest of the evening. A couple of my best friends from elementary school arrived and that was a great comfort to me. The Word of God is most definitely true. I found that laughter or a merry heart was like a medicine, as stated in Proverbs 17:22. That laughter provided temporary relief and almost a brief escape from the pain of the blow.

Initially, after the surgery, people weren't allowed to see him because of the sensitivity of his condition. We couldn't go into Timothy's room because the neurologist wanted his brain to heal. Because his brain couldn't be stimulated in any way, I blocked all outside visitors. We (the kids and I) did go in briefly. Quietly, we stood without speaking or trying to wake him, and when they were gone, I would silently go in to check on him. I would stand there and silently pray. Other than our children, only one other couple—one pastor friend and his wife from out of town—saw him. I didn't want to compromise his health any further, so I strictly followed the neurologist's instructions.

Once word got out, I decided to activate a privacy code so that no one could visit him without my permission. People attempted to visit but were turned away. I felt that they were there to take a look. They didn't even stop by to check on me— and they had to pass me in the waiting room to get to his room. From my perspective, this wasn't a normal visitation or spectating type of situation. In my mind, I was protecting him from the public who just wanted the 411 in order to gossip. This was a life or death private family matter, and I was going to do everything in my power to protect him. Although I believed he would pull through, this was a moment-by-moment, day-by-day battle. He had to survive.

A few days later, one couple who had attended the church here and there lied to the nursing staff to gain entry. This was the following Sunday. By that time, I was sleeping in a lounge chair in his room and, of course, hadn't gone to service. When the woman entered first, I became extremely upset at being caught off guard. Before I knew it, she had walked over to my lounge chair to greet me. I immediately got up and graciously walked her out. Then the guy came in. I felt violated. I learned later from the nursing staff that they had lied about whom they were going to visit. I have no idea how they got his room number, and they are exactly what I was trying to protect my husband from—people coming in to "take a look."

While people were talking, speculating, being curious, gossiping, etc., my posture was different having been Timothy's wife of nearly twenty-eight years. I just longed for the love of my life to be whole again. I wanted my shattered life to be put back together... to see light at the end of the tunnel... and for this nightmare to only be a dream.

NOT OUT OF THE WOODS YET

Little did I know that our time in ICU would be touch and go, life or death. By the evening of the day that I considered a breakthrough with his temperature regulated, he had caught pneumonia. It was then that I realized this battle was not even close to being over. All I could focus on was him pulling through. There was no life outside of the ICU for me although everyone else had to continue theirs. I was in a totally different, unfamiliar place where everything had changed. I hadn't even had time to process what had happened, to mourn, to think about what the future might hold, to think about myself.

I was there watching and praying; that is all I had the strength to do. Because the work week had begun, I was alone, except for when I would get a visitor here or there. Timothy's mom and a close relative came to visit that week, another pastor friend visited from out of town, and my children kept me company here and there.

Due to the onset of pneumonia Sunday night, by Monday afternoon (day four), they advised me that they wanted to perform another surgery to install a trach to help him with his breathing. Following the surgery, they had to suction out through the trach all the fluid that had accumulated in his lungs. This was traumatic for me to watch and a horrible experience for him as he would violently cough in response to the procedure. They performed this several times a day around the clock. I felt bad for him having to undergo it. I didn't understand. And all I had strength to do was pray and empathize with the suffering he was enduring. You wouldn't have wished that on your worst enemy.

Being in his room 24/7 was unnerving. I would see all his numbers when his blood pressure was elevated again (around 200 over 100-plus) and the medical professionals as they fought to get it regulated. I would hear the machines making noises throughout the night, and I became familiar with each sound. By Thursday, they put a lounge chair in his room where I slept—once it was okay to be in his room—that was much more comfortable than the waiting room bench.

46 THE DAY My Life Changed

The days began to bleed into each other. I couldn't help but take one day at a time. About five days in, I remember telling the Lord, *I can't take this. It's too much. I can't live this out moment by moment, buzzer by buzzer, alarm by alarm.* That was wearing me out more than anything. I had to mentally and emotionally set my gauge farther out to beyond that one day at a time. I read my Bible for words of comfort, even though it was hard to lock in and focus on God's Holy Word. My mind was in a fog as I dealt with my emotions and the daily necessities of his care.

The days began to bleed into each other. I couldn't help but take one day at a time, moment by moment.

I hadn't gone home yet due to his volatile condition. My daughter had brought me clean clothes and toiletries as I lived there with him. I didn't even have the mental capacity to be in tune with what ministry my children needed at that time. I knew they were old enough to take care of their basic needs, but I can't imagine what they felt like with neither parent present.

I felt like I was living in two dimensions. With my natural eyes, I was looking at a "jacked-up" situation yet believing for full recovery with my spiritual eyes. It was during that time alone with my husband that my expectation of his full recovery was birthed. Just like in our daily lives, things in the natural world can look pretty bleak (especially these days).

However, faith takes a person beyond the things that are seen to the spiritual world where expectations can be realized and new realities can be birthed.

I really can't say that the Lord told me to believe for full recovery. That expectancy was born out of my knowledge of God as a healer, His desire for us to believe His Word, and even the Word's instructions that we pray for the sick to be healed. I felt that my posture of belief is what God expects us to do in all circumstances, no matter how long it may take to manifest. I couldn't embrace any other reality. I couldn't see God *not* answering my prayer or taking us all the way through this circumstance, like He had done for me in the past. I knew I had to set myself on what I felt would be victory in order to endure.

Once Timothy woke up around day five or six, he saw me in the lounge chair and winked his eye. That became his morning ritual. It warmed my heart and gave me hope that my husband was still in there. It meant the world to me that he had the presence of mind to affectionately communicate with me even though he couldn't speak with the trach. I would smile, just like when we first met, because he had always brought me laughter. He knew that even if I wasn't pleased with him, he could make me laugh and ease the tension. I couldn't wait to tell our children when they visited. They, too, shared in my excitement.

One evening, I was in the hallway, and I ran into a male nurse who knew of my husband. We ended up discussing my husband's condition, as I still sought to understand what the recovery process would be. The nurse explained that when people "return" from that type of stroke, they can have a totally different personality. I listened intently as he spoke, but I maintained my expectation. I believe that with God, all things are possible to him that believes.

THE SECOND TRAUMA

I want to share another experience so that you can understand the various dynamics of my trauma in the ICU. One of my visitors mentioned a conversation with a hospital employee. That employee disclosed to my visitor some facts about my husband's medical condition that I hadn't heard. It felt like someone had stabbed me with a knife and was waiting for me to bleed out. This was the epitome of violation on all levels: personal, pastoral, legal due to HIPAA privacy laws, etc. She confronted the person by reminding her that it was illegal to go into a patient's medical records, as well as a violation of the hospital's rules, and that she should not have done that.

I looked further into this for several reasons. I wanted to see if the information was true and if I had any recourse. I asked Timothy's nurse to tell me what his chart said. She explained that it said he was in a "coma-like state." This confirmed that his file had been illegally viewed because the person had described him as being in a "coma." I hadn't received that news, so I was shocked; imagine hearing such private, sensitive information in the streets, so to speak, or in the gossip circles. I felt that blow big time, and I was deeply hurt, angry, and disappointed, especially with people who consider themselves Christians.

I had an investigation run on everyone who had viewed Timothy's records who wasn't directly involved in his care. I was allowed to see a list of around eleven people to determine if I knew them. Some were former members of our church, others were relatives of former members, while there were other names with which I wasn't familiar. Do people really do this type of unethical, hurtful stuff to their patients, let alone a pastor? I was totally outdone. I had worked tirelessly around the clock to protect him, yet it wasn't enough. No one deserves that type of violation—that prying into their private matters. I was traumatized on top of the trauma I was already bearing.

I was told that my only recourse was to have them personally interviewed and fired if they couldn't explain why they were in his medical file. I thought long and hard about what I should do. I wanted them reprimanded because I would hate to see someone else be violated by hospital employees as we were. I struggled with the fact that they would lose their jobs if they were found to be in violation. I decided to show mercy and not pursue it any further. They got their nosy or gossip itch scratched, but "God will be my defender" is the position I took. He will repay. The damage had been done. I had to depend on God to heal my already shattered heart.

MY MELTDOWN

Yet, I managed to maintain my own personal strength until a literal meltdown occurred without my permission. A few friends of mine—who were also pastors' wives—contacted me to schedule a visit at the hospital since that had become my temporary dwelling place. I thought I was prepared as I left the room, walked out of the ICU and down the relatively long hallway to the waiting room, went in, and greeted them. To my surprise, I opened my mouth to speak, but tears began to flow instead. I couldn't even fight them back, although I had previously thought of myself as being pretty good at maintaining my composure.

Strength is just a part of my normal personality, as people often speak of me as being strong. My parents told me that I had a very strong will; actually, they described me as being more stubborn than they were. When I was a baby, they were determined not to have me sleep in their bed, but I would cry until I won and then giggle afterward when they picked me up to put me in their bed. They said I won every time, no matter how determined they were to deny me the privilege of sleeping with them. That's where they formed that opinion of me being stubborn and able to do whatever I set my mind to achieve.

Sports will toughen you up as well because of the rigors of training and competition—you literally can't be weak. The principles I had formerly acquired in athletics were applied to all of my life situations. My body and character had been built by athletics, and I have possessed a strong belief in Christ from my youth. Of course, having very strong-willed parents, it was in my DNA as well.

To be considered weak was not my M.O., but in that moment of vulnerability, I didn't care that my weakness was apparent to all. This was me being human, not a superhero. My pain couldn't help but seep through, revealing the effects of multiple days of standing in the gap with no real rest, let alone sleep. My mind was foggy, and I had unanswered questions—all while trying to maintain the role I had played for years, standing strongly by Timothy's side as "a helper suitable." This was the real deal, nothing fake about it—real trauma, real pain, and the real need for understanding were what my tears conveyed that day.

For years, my husband and I had ministered to countless people in their times of tragedy, helping them put the shattered pieces of their lives back together—never anticipating that this kind of calamity would befall us also. My ministry peers shared that moment with me and lovingly prayed for me, assuring me that they were there for support.

THE MIRACLE

Day by day, I watched the initial healing process: the removal of bandages and staples in his head, all the doctors' and resident assistant visits, and the initial physical therapy. His first physical therapy session was mind-blowing; it's where I saw just how far he would have to go to gain my expected full recovery. The physical therapist literally had to hold him up in an attempt to exercise him because he couldn't do anything on his own. I had never seen anything like this. I guess I had at least expected him to be able to sit up, but I didn't realize his right side wasn't functional. He could move his leg a little, but his arm had no life at all. When he had first awakened, the kids and I put a pen in his hand to see if he could write, and he just scribbled some lines. My thinking was, *Well, that will come back too.* I held my composure, but inside I was devastated yet still trying to hold on to hope.

As the therapy session progressed, I couldn't believe what I was witnessing. In nearly all the situations in which I had witnessed him, strength was the aroma my husband emitted as he stood in people's presence. I'm certain that I was deeply traumatized. Where does a person put this? How does one process it? I had no frame of reference. Nothing in life had prepared me for this moment. While it was just as life-threatening, my cancer experience seemed to be totally different to me. In retrospect, maybe it was because I was on the other side watching him this time.

Where was the miracle? Well, I came to grips with the fact that a literal miracle had occurred in his survival alone. On the day of his departure to rehab, the physician assistant (an African American young lady) came to the room radiating with joy and delight. I couldn't help but ask, "Why are you so happy?" She proceeded to inform me that my husband had been the topic of discussion at their staff meetings, being that most people don't survive a major stroke such as his.

A blood clot had traveled from his heart through the main artery and cut off the oxygen supply to the brain. The MRI showed a large section of the left side of his brain was affected, and that area is what houses the speech center. I learned that later. Initially, all I had been told was that "the damage had been done." They didn't talk specifics about whether he would walk or if he could talk; that was all a discovery as the journey progressed.

Where was the miracle?

It took two months for it to finally hit me as to what "the damage" really was that the neurologist had previously described. I discovered that the assistant, along with the neurologist and her team, was elated that he had survived. I learned that death was generally the outcome from their experience with that type of stroke. Up to this point, we had only discussed what the plan was for his survival. Now, I was made aware of the staff's outlook—this was a miracle. I know that it was the prayers of the people of God, family, and friends nationwide that affected this outcome. Personally, I was so locked into his recovery that I hadn't considered him dying. Although I knew his condition was very serious, death wasn't a possibility that I would allow my mind to even consider.

At the beginning of this journey, it came to me to capture it through journaling. I journaled for about a year straight. Here is what I wrote on day four:

Monday was full of visits and the handling of administrative things to make sure that everything was in place to move the ministry forward in our absence. Needless to say, I was totally exhausted as the last guest left at 10 p.m. My husband was pretty stable at the time. The hospital staff set me up in their family suite, but I still couldn't sleep. My daughter, Amber, was with me that night. To our surprise, the next day we discovered that the room was full of bed bugs, so we had to leave.

I decided that I had to cut my visits because it was too exhausting to visit all day, then be up at night checking on his progress. The doctor told us not to stimulate his brain because she wanted his brain to heal. I allowed Beverly Towns (our chief intercessor at the ministry) in the room to pray silently, and I would sit silently when I was in the room. He was asleep during that time; he hadn't awakened.

The medical staff was still battling to regulate his blood pressure. The swelling of the brain after surgery had begun, as the neurologist had advised me in our first conversation about the need for surgery. He had tubes all over his body keeping him alive and was not really recognizable at this point. However, he was still that man whom I deeply loved. I still felt that it was an uphill journey because things in the natural world didn't look good. I took courage in that he's a strong man in every way. I knew he would fight with us.

The doctor's report was that he was progressing according to her expectations. Often, I would ask her about things I heard from the nurses, and her response was, "In the grand scheme of things he is headed in the right direction." She kept her focus on the big picture and expressed that she wasn't concerned about the lesser things. This gave me perspective because I was concerned about it all! From then on, I reset my focus to look at the "grand scheme of things."

I remember sitting in his room watching his blood pressure fluctuate from moment to moment. It was gruesome and tiring to do that. Then I decided I couldn't do this… I decided I had to set myself up for the outcome I expected in the end because it was overwhelming to judge his condition moment by moment. Things were always shifting in terms of the numbers, counts, and beeps of the machines. One nurse, Allen, advised me to assess things on a weekly basis. That really helped me attempt to look farther out.

CHAPTER FOUR
I Am Not Alone

WILL HE RECOVER?

"The goal is to get him into rehab as quickly as possible since we now know he's going to survive," said the neurologist a couple of days prior to his release on day eleven. Her statement again left me pondering her words: "Since we now know he's going to survive." This came directly from her, not her assistant this time, confirming the miracle of his survival. I guess they really didn't expect him to pull through, or this was at least not the norm, as the physician assistant had indicated. She (the physician assistant) even went as far as to say, "It was the Lord that he survived." Obviously, she was a believer even though I didn't ask. I definitely agreed with her but didn't have the medical perspective that supported her belief.

Divine intervention had taken place and was evident to all. I had only known from a perspective of faith that "this was God." Nonetheless, those words were refreshing to hear coming from medical personnel. I joined in on the celebration as I tucked her words into my heart for encouragement. I don't even recall my expression changing outwardly to match her joy. I was beyond exhausted emotionally, physically, and spiritually. However, it gave me hope for the days ahead. He had survived, indeed, and the journey of recovery began. I wasn't given much time to select a facility for rehab, and the one I wanted him to go to didn't receive patients with a trach. So, he ended up at a different facility by default from March 24 to July 31. The question now was, would he recover?

I AM NOT ALONE

The fact that I was not alone had to be established from the onset because I felt as alone as I ever have in my life. During this part of the journey, while I was still in a fog mentally and emotionally, the song "I Am Not Alone" by Kari Jobe became my anthem. My daughter had introduced me to that song. Not only did I listen to it daily as I drove to and from the nursing home (a 25-minute ride one way), it became a source of life. It was my constant reminder that God was still nearby. I refused to believe anything else, for I had come to know Him as a God who will neither leave nor forsake His people . . . as a God who comes alongside us even in our trials . . . as a God who comforts us in our sufferings and distress.

> *I had come to know Him as a God who will never leave nor forsake His people . . . as a God who comes alongside us even in our trials . . . as a God who comforts our sufferings and distress.*

I listened, sang along in worship, and allowed the tears to flow. I sang and cried, sang and cried, and sang and cried. Even late at night when I arrived home each day, I sat on my chaise lounge and sang and cried. Not having the words to express myself to the Lord, I knew that He, being the All-Knowing God, could interpret my tears and worship—they were all I had to give. That was my therapy.

Even though I sang that I was not alone, in reality, I felt alone. Daily, I was alone for the nursing home visits (unless my children visited with me some evenings). I didn't even realize I had left my 13-year-old son at home all summer because I was attending to his dad. I tried to bear the burden of the trauma by myself to enable the kids to continue on with their lives because they were young. And we didn't allow visitors because of the nature of Timothy's injury. With half of his skull cap off, I didn't want people to see him in that condition, and I'm sure he wouldn't have desired that either. So, in that sense, I felt alone and the need to remain in protection mode.

I also felt alone in that everyone else got an opportunity to continue with their lives, and my life was shattered. I'm not saying people didn't care or wouldn't have helped in whatever way possible. It is just different when it's you who is wearing the shoes, or it's your journey to tread. No one can bear that for you. One thing I was certain of is that my theological view of God was still intact. He promised to be with us, and I took Him at His Word, clinging to Him for dear life.

THE DAY *My Life Changed*

THE HORRORS OF THE NURSING HOME STAY

If you have never had to be in a nursing home or have a relative there, consider yourself blessed. I learned from the senior staff that people go there to die. They see so much death that it is a relief to rehab and release patients. *Wow,* is all I could think concerning that statement, being that my husband was a new patient. I guess that was encouragement in hindsight. *The hospital sends patients to a place of death to rehab*, was my first thought.

Would he recover? Was the staff equipped to get him through this phase of the journey? A nursing home didn't resemble what I thought of when I thought of a rehab facility. Now, I felt the need to oversee his care because I didn't really trust their qualifications. I immediately found them incapable of handling his dietary needs since he was a vegetarian. One meal was a plate full of lettuce. I thought, *this is crazy.* Since the meal options were horrible, I asked the staff to pay me for groceries (because I knew his insurance was covering the cost of his meals) so that I could prepare his meals. They admitted they weren't equipped to handle his dietary needs and agreed to these arrangements. I would arrive in the morning to bring his breakfast, stay through lunch, and return to either bring dinner or ensure he received a proper meal. In an attempt to have something on hand for him to eat, they purchased his vegetarian patties. More often than not, I brought dinner too. His mom brought meals when she visited from Lansing as well.

I was literally at the nursing home two to three times every single day. My children and mother-in-law would relieve me of one of the visits here and there. I returned home daily, only to rest and begin again the next morning. I had no personal time to process what had happened or to think about my mental, physical, emotional, or spiritual needs. I hadn't, in the least bit, recovered from the eleven-day hospital stay, and now we had the daily journey of rehab and healing ahead of us.

At this point, I had more questions than answers. How's the family holding up? How is the ministry holding up? Many people wanted answers that I didn't have. What's the time frame of his recovery? Can he talk? He still had the trach, so I didn't know. I actually assumed that he could. Those types of questions put tremendous pressure on me because I didn't have answers, only pain. Deep within me, I hoped people would have the sensitivity and maturity to allow me to speak when I had something to say. I now understand why high-profile people request privacy. Everything isn't for public display. Families need private time to handle private matters. This was not only unexpected but altogether new to me, so all I could do was handle this journey day by day.

THE BATTLE FOR PROPER CARE

A few weeks into rehab, I recognized that part of my stress resulted from me unknowingly shouldering the burden of feeling the need to present him back to the church and community "recovered," so we could resume our normal lives. At some point, I decided that it wasn't my burden to heal him, thus releasing myself from this daunting task.

> *At some point, I decided that it wasn't my burden to heal him, thus releasing myself from this daunting task.*

I was not only there to ensure his nutritional care but his physical therapy as well. I wanted to see what the process would be and how he was progressing. I wanted to make sure they were taking him to therapy daily. Once, I was there early on a Sunday morning until the afternoon. I expected them to do his therapy. After inquiring the next day with staff, I was told they came to do his therapy. I insisted that they hadn't because I was there. It was that type of circumstance that caused me not to be confident that he was really being properly cared for and kept me in battle mode.

I knew that they weren't miracle workers, but I wanted them to do their job in aiding his recovery process. I know that they see so many patients, and one patient may not take priority over the other. I just wanted them to give him the best they had to offer.

Once, I returned for my normal evening visit, and I had the door closed as usual. He heard one of the aides speaking outside his door, and he pointed to the door with a look of disgust toward her. I knew she had done something that he really didn't like, but because he couldn't communicate, I couldn't find out what the offense was. His response was clear, though; she had done something that wasn't good.

HOW IS THE FAMILY HOLDING UP?

One evening on my return home, I had a family huddle with my children. It was a time to checked in on the kids to see how they were doing, as well as to have a time of prayer that we were accustomed to at the day's end—I called it family prayer. During one particular family huddle, Timothy, our youngest son, had his first real meltdown. He talked about a close classmate's brother who had a minor surgery and some other things that happened that day in school, and then in the same breath said, "And Dad had a stroke." He then broke down sobbing as his big brother and sister each sat by his side, consoling him. I was on my chaise lounge, letting the tears flow while feeling helpless to make it better. That moment exposed the glaring reality that we were missing the strong man who had guided our family spiritually, who was a great provider and loved by his family.

Timothy still refers to the stroke as the day he "lost his dad," even though his dad is yet alive. It also broke my heart when I had my eldest son visit the nursing home one evening to relieve me, and the next morning the nurse shared with me that he had left the room crying. Dad was their "hero," and I wasn't bothered by that; I wanted them to have a strong relationship with him—especially being sons.

My kids mostly kept their pain silent—they held it within. A couple of them, being introverted, retreated further within themselves; my youngest clung to his friend group. My middle son, who considers things from a philosophical perspective, pondered the question, "What happened?" He is the one who likes to look at things from what he considers "reality." And when we were treating my husband normally—as if he hadn't had a stroke, Emmanuel told us, "Dad is different." Yes, their dad was away at the nursing home; I was away attending to his needs.

On Fridays, we would have our normal family day there at the nursing home. We played games and laughed together; that time at least represented a resemblance of the life we once shared as a family. My children, like their dad, are very humorous. I was accustomed to years of laughter in my home because of their silly behavior that often brought all of us to tears of joy. Once, we were on vacation in Canada, and something happened that was so funny we all laughed for at least thirty minutes nonstop. Our sides ached, and we had to run to the bathroom to avoid an accident.

HE'S PROGRESSING

A nursing home is a sad place; even the administrative staff expressed that reality. If there were any other place of privacy that I could have taken him, I would have. Timothy's reputation as a pastor had already preceded him upon his arrival. He hated being there with a passion, but I knew it was his best option. He had to be under medical care to regain his strength, and I wasn't qualified to care for him at this point. Towards the end of his four-month stay, he was strong enough for me to check him out and bring him home during the day. He absolutely loved it! It was interesting; on his first ride home, we passed by the church. He looked and pointed to it. He's very observant and totally aware of his surroundings. He's the type that will notice anything new being built or changes being made to stores or structures that I would pass by every day and not pay any attention to.

I was still watching his progress, sitting in on all the therapy sessions, observing while being educated about his condition. The day arrived when the trach came out, literally—this was actually early on during his stay. It came out on its own, so they sent him back to the hospital for observation of his breathing. They decided it could remain out and no surgery was needed; that was a good thing. I was excited because the moment arrived when I would see whether or not he could speak. That was the most important thing in all of this; his entire life depended on him speaking.

When he returned without the trach, and he was unable to speak, I experienced the second most devastating moment in this journey—I was faced with the fact that he couldn't speak, and I didn't know what to do with that. It was obvious that he understood everything I was saying, his personality was the same, he was even the same jokester. He looked the same (other than his skull cap missing); what was up with this? Was this for real?

It was on my way home that day that it dawned on me what "the damage" was that had been done. Wow! If you think I was dumbfounded before, now, I was even more so. How will he recover? The magnitude of change went to soaring heights. Would I ever hear my husband's voice again? He's a teacher of the Word of God; would he ever return to the pulpit?

What about the counsel and wisdom his children needed from him in this stage of their lives? The books yet unwritten ... the sermons unpreached ... the television program he was preparing to launch... and the church members who would always need his voice? His mom, who had served the Lord all her life, was believing for his recovery. His friends looked to him for wisdom and guidance. What about the leadership he'd provided the city and his wife who longed to hear, "I love you"? Absolute devastation. I am certain of that now. Who could bear this?

I had learned of a younger patient at that nursing home who survived a stroke of lesser severity and had walked out of the facility. I immediately set that as a goal for Timothy, and my husband, just over four months later, was able to walk out of the facility—his family and his therapists by his side, cheering and crying. He had a walker, but that didn't matter. He was still on his way to recovery in my mind and had come a long way from the condition he was in when he arrived. That was a day of victory for us! I would take all that I could get at this point to fuel my hope.

Time was still a critical factor in his recovery, so I learned from the therapist. I was ready for the next phase with expectation that, in due season, we would witness the rest of this miraculous story. There was even a Christian doctor at the facility who confirmed that my husband had already recovered further than most people who experienced that type of stroke. In his assessment, full recovery was a possibility.

CHAPTER FIVE
The Journey to Recovery

*P*eople's versions of our story that have passed from mouth to mouth can only contain a minute portion of the total picture. They had to take a piece of information, far removed from the actual facts, and fill in the blanks because they didn't have first-hand information. Hearsay is always distorted, with details lost or embellished, misinformed, and subjective while leading to false conclusions. As a journalism student, I was trained to get the facts from the source. I have learned not to run with what I hear. There's another part of my character that believes the best. I don't glory in others' calamity. I had first-hand information, and this is my time to tell it.

HOME SWEET HOME, OR IS IT?

To this day, I often look at my husband, hoping he won't catch me staring. In my mind, I'm saying, *My husband had a stroke.* I can't say that it has settled in, even though it's been more than seven years. Yet, I am still believing that any day could be the day for his speech to break forth. The neurologist had given me hope when she told him, "Keep trying to speak because sometimes the right side of the brain helps the left side of the brain, creating a path for the language to flow." What? That's all I needed to fuel my prayer. I made it my aim to ask the Lord to allow a path to open from the right side of his brain to the left to enable the language to flow. I have noticed, over time, various words slipping out to my surprise.

    The day arrived when he came home from the nursing home. I quickly realized that I should have taken the advice of the nursing staff and doctors, who told me that I should rest because it would be more demanding when he returned home. Boy, were they right. I now wish I could rewind the clock and trust that he would be okay without my daily presence. As I explained, I had meticulously overseen his care and was still operating on very little rest and no self-care.

    It wasn't an hour before the reality of the new demand on me was evident. His medical bed was stationed on the lower level in our family room. The bathroom is by the front door, which is quite a distance to walk. His mode of transportation was his wheelchair, but he needed full assistance until he could gain his strength. I was up and down, up and down, up and down, taking him back and forth to the restroom. After about the fourth time of this, I soon realized that I wasn't going to survive this demanding routine; I just couldn't bear it. I was actually getting frustrated; I was past exhaustion. Therefore, I decided to let him go ahead of me, so I could sit for a couple minutes. While I waited until he was in the bathroom, I heard him fall to the floor. Imagine how I felt as I ran to his rescue. This was horrible!

Boy, how my life had changed! The reality was yet unfolding—from wife to caregiver at ages fifty-four and fifty, really? It would be different if we were in our eighties or nineties. This couldn't be happening. Where does a person even begin with processing this calamity? What part of my life was left intact? Nothing. Everything had changed in a huge way. We had survived many hardships and trials. We had even slain some giants along the way, but this battle for sure trumped them all. Nothing about this journey was sweet. We still lived in the same house, so our surroundings were familiar, but our lives were drastically affected. This was totally unfamiliar territory. Once again, I could only take life one day at a time.

Everything had changed in a huge way. We had survived many hardships and trials. We had even slain some giants along the way, but this battle for sure trumped them all.

HOW IS THE CHURCH HOLDING UP?

I wasn't prepared for the ministry to be shaken to the extent that it was. People began to ease out the door—some immediately, others over time. Others waited just long enough to see what Timothy's recovery would be; then, they too found a reason to jump ship. No one, not even I, could fill my husband's shoes. I get that, but it still hurt terribly as I saw families that he had sacrificed his life for seemingly forsaking us when we needed them the most. Of course, that's not how they saw it, but that's what it felt like to my family and me.

God is faithful! I will believe that until the day that I die. Even though we may not understand life's circumstances, I know where my help comes from. There were people who decided they were going to stay and fight with us. As one of our intercessors always says, "The remnant is strong." These, too, were people whom he had shepherded for years through all of their tough seasons and struggles. Some he had counseled... married them... and was at the hospital when they delivered their children. One guy, who was a founding member of the ministry, experienced a death in his family. My daughter and I rushed to the hospital to be by his and his wife's side, and he commented, "Pastor has always been there for my family." That day, my daughter and I had to represent him. Those words were a testament to my husband's dedication to the people.

Every leader at the ministry was either homegrown or groomed by my husband as he trained leaders for ministry through our Bible college. Everyone would admit that my husband was a brilliant teacher and outstanding trainer. Some people say those who go through our ministry training can serve as pastors in other local ministries because of how well-equipped they are. Had they not received that training, they may not have made it. The leadership team stepped up and did what we had been trained to do, which made the transition much easier. I had no other choice than to leave it in

God's hands because I had no ability to carry the ministry, my husband, and my family all at the same time.

THE GAME CHANGER

I can still see the serious expression on my middle son's face as he stepped in front of me while I was walking down the upstairs hallway. I was on my way downstairs to attend to my husband again. I couldn't help but stop in my tracks because he had impeded my pathway as he had slid directly in front of me. Looking at me face-to-face and eye to eye, he commented in a direct but loving way, "Mom, I don't like seeing you like this." I didn't know what "like this" looked like in his eyes, but I quickly got the message.

That encounter was another profound moment when change had forced its way into view. I had to listen because in my mind, the kids couldn't afford to lose both parents—one to illness, the other as a vulnerable, overwhelmed caregiver. Prior to that moment, I hadn't even taken the time to process the thing that was so obvious to him as an onlooker. I just kept pushing, doing what was necessary to hold everything together (or so I thought). In all of this, I was yet hoping that things would be better in the days ahead. I was working hard towards the moment when life would return to "normal." Well, I didn't totally want the normal back because I knew some things were out of balance, but I would gladly exchange that for this. I'm confident, with hindsight, we could have made the necessary adjustments.

After the moment of my son's loving confrontation, I vividly remember telling the Lord in my heart, *If I can't do this by Your grace, then it won't be done.* That was my admittance to being incapable of handling my trauma on my own. Deciding to depend on God's grace opened new access to God. I had previously unknowingly handled life in my own strength. This time, although I have broad shoulders because of my administrative gifting, I concluded that I couldn't carry anything else. I was literally forced to learn to live with divine assistance—no matter how menial the task.

I was reminded of that time I literally wrestled to get him up off the bathroom floor and into the wheelchair for at least thirty minutes to no avail. I stopped and prayed, *Holy Spirit, please help me pick my husband up off the floor.* Within a couple of minutes Timothy was back in the chair, and I know it was the Lord. We had tried that maneuver before, and it hadn't worked. That's what I mean when I say, "It had to be grace." I thought, *How many other times in my life have I not just stopped and asked for help?* If it was that easy, I needed to really make that a way of life. Grace was a game changer! With this refresher course in grace, my strategy was to use it as the vehicle for us to overcome this enormous obstacle.

THE NEW NORM (THERAPY)

To my surprise, my husband was able to receive at-home physical therapy, occupational therapy, and speech therapy. After he utilized all of the insurance coverage, I located other therapists to work with him. I even hired some at-home exercise and massage therapists who came several times a week. Though this was costly, I wanted him to have the maximum opportunity to recover. Insurance companies don't give adequate coverage for major strokes—only thirty visits per year. The mindset of the insurance company is to deny coverage if the patient isn't making progress. It's absolutely a catch-22. Patients may not make the kinds of advances that insurance companies are willing to pay for, but if they don't have therapy, they will regress. This is a horrible evil that leaves families stuck in a rut; most can only afford so much.

Family life pretty much revolved around Timothy's needs 24/7. This was the new norm. When he needed something, one of us ran to his side to give him the help he needed. It was tough for us all. Everyone dealt with it the best that they knew how. We all played a part in helping, though certain aspects were very challenging for the kids. Again, I tried to bear the brunt of the load, leaving them with the lighter responsibilities. I formerly had to care for my mother when she was sick, so I understand what the psyche goes through when the roles are reversed. At least, then, I was in my mid-thirties which made it a little easier to cope with.

For me, I dare not attempt to play the role of a dad and a mom; I know I'm not equipped to do that. The boys were more aloof, but Amber, our only daughter ("Daddy's girl"), still drew near, at least making an attempt to receive the love, nurturing, and affirmation to which she was accustomed. In the fall of the same year, she left for college. This was huge because she was the first of our children to leave home. The others had attended school locally up to that point. As we held hands to pray, her dad began to cry. Laughingly, we all called him a big baby.

HOLDING IT ALL TOGETHER

I was the glue, the one who pretty much held it all together. However, Amber returned home on the weekends to relieve me during her first year of college. The following year, my middle son left for college. They attended Michigan State University and lived in the same dorm, so I was relieved at least they had each other. That year, they rarely returned home because my son decided he wasn't going to come home on weekends like Amber had previously done. So, I adjusted and handled it. It was my goal for them to go on with their lives. I didn't want them to suffer regret later in life because they didn't get to live their lives. I wanted to protect them from that burden.

Our eldest son, Brendon, graduated from college in May 2016, so, even though he lived at home, he was busy with work in a new engineering position. The youngest, Timothy, was busy with schoolwork and activities. By the year's end, I had stepped into the lead pastor role at the ministry that we had started, hoping to advance the work while my husband was on the sidelines recovering. I was advised by my mentors to do so because of the grace of God on my life to lead. I believe that I am a natural leader, but the days ahead presented an enormous opportunity to navigate through even more murky waters of change.

Yet recovery is happening. With time, Timothy has become strong enough to regain independence. The main things we need to provide now are his meals, showers, therapy, and outings for his enjoyment. I'm attempting to provide him with as much "normalcy" as possible. He has always known the exact time for his meds and what meds he should take; I just lay them out for him. For exercise, he walks (with a walker) laps around the house, traveling from upstairs to the basement and back. As an avid sports fan, he definitely knows how to work the sports channels. He's in tune with everything that goes on in the house—even my phone conversations.

He participates in family and ministry decisions as before. I've endeavored to allow him to maintain headship in the areas that he's able to. Often, putting myself in his shoes, I think of how horrific this is for him, trying to alleviate frustration due to the lack of verbal communication. Having been married thirty-five years now, I know the routines and can pretty much figure out anything that he wants. I am very grateful for the sharpness of his mind. In my research, I've discovered that most people die from a massive stroke, especially males, while others don't recover nearly to the place that he has already. That is a blessing! Instead of thinking of what I have lost, I focus on what I am thankful for because, as bad as it is, it could have been worse. That's my perspective.

He's been able to attend three of his children's college graduations and witness his youngest son complete high school as class valedictorian, which is what he knew he could achieve. He had told Timothy years prior that he could achieve that goal if he wanted to because he was keenly aware of Timothy's intellectual potential. Timothy is now a senior at Michigan State University, on schedule to graduate in May 2023. Praise the Lord for His grace! Even though it seems like I am holding things together, I realize just like the famous poem "Footprints" says that it was the Lord carrying me when there was only one set of footprints in the sand.

YET STILL I STAND

I once heard a famous preacher speak of going through a storm in his life. He said as he walked across the stage to grab the mic, he didn't know if he was going to collapse under the weight of his circumstances. His knees had almost buckled. I can literally say, "I feel you." Just standing is major, let alone walking. Preaching on top of that has to be divine. I understand when the Apostle Paul felt forsaken by all and was able to confidently perceive that the Lord stood by him. This is and was my hope: "I will stand as long as You are upholding me, Lord. Even in the middle of the storm, I will continue in the assignment You have on my life."

Even in the middle of the storm, I will continue in the assignment You have on my life.

When I say it takes every ounce of strength that you have internally to stand, I am not exaggerating. It doesn't even make sense from a natural standpoint to continue, even though I was trained as a champion athlete, and I have often declared that "there is no quit in me." That statement in and of itself has been tested to its limit. Unbeknownst to me, my standing would encourage so many people who could only imagine what it took for me to stand; one person even told me that I didn't look like I needed help. I couldn't believe what I was hearing. "Well, that was far from the truth," I explained. That had to be grace she was witnessing. Just waking up was a chore, getting a good night's rest was a battle, having mental clarity was precious, and preparing myself to minister was like war.

CHAPTER SIX
The Impact

EVERYTHING HAS CHANGED

About two years into the recovery journey, I hosted our annual women's conference. I informed my guest speaker of my husband's stroke. She had experience in counseling, and I will never forget her words: "This is huge." She kept repeating them as she stared me in the eyes in an attempt to make sure that her message was resonating. I stared back, intently soaking her words in so that I could make sure I was living in reality. She mentioned that it had affected every area of my life and that I needed to make sure I went to therapy to help me sort through things. I agreed, and when I went to my first appointment, I texted her for accountability.

Therapy didn't last long, not because it wasn't needed, but somehow, I got off track early on and never returned. It took every waking moment to handle my daily responsibilities. During the first year of my husband's speech therapy, we traveled forty-five minutes one way, three times a week. Had I known better, I would have continued in therapy for my mental and emotional health.

> *It took every waking moment to handle my daily responsibilities.*

Everything had indeed changed, and my guest speaker was absolutely correct, "This is huge." I was and still am experiencing uncharted territory relationally, mentally, emotionally, and spiritually. I had known who we were prior to the stroke, but I had to become acquainted with our new selves. There is no way you can survive this level of trauma and not experience personal change. Your life will go in one direction or the other—a breakdown or transformation. I chose to be transformed. My prevailing belief was that the Lord would work things together for our good (Romans 8:28).

GRIEVING THE LOSS

About five years into my journey, I met another therapist who helped me process the trauma. She got my attention because she said she had worked on her soul, in regards to inner healing, every day for more than thirty years. I remember thinking, *What does that look like?* I knew I hadn't been intentional about working on my soul. I concentrated on my spirit and body through the exercise I managed to resume. I decided to seek her counsel, and during our first appointment, I experienced another meltdown when she said, "My concern is that you haven't taken the time to grieve the loss." She concurred that this was "huge" and that I had suffered loss in every area.

I had not thought of my life in terms of what I had "lost" because I just kept moving forward in hopes that I would see the light at the end of the tunnel someday. When I heard those words, tears began to flow down my cheek. I got a glimpse of what the loss actually was; it was staring me in my face. It was enormous, unspeakable loss. I'm sure she could hear the sniffles as the tears became more intense to the point that I could no longer speak because I had to gather myself. This was shocking to me because I thought I had cried all the tears that I had. New, fresh tears, as if I hadn't cried before, were gushing out as if a door had been opened and what was being held behind it had broken through.

I was a wreck, and I wasn't prepared for that moment; she recommended that I take a week off and go somewhere to be alone and just grieve. I took her up on it, because at that point, I couldn't stop crying. I contacted the elders at the church to inform them of my need, again, as the tears were still rolling. They understood and agreed to do whatever was necessary to carry the ministry in my absence. My daughter helped at home while I was gone. I packed my bags and drove to a hotel in Grand Rapids, Michigan, about two hours away. Checking into the hotel, I put my bags down, laid on the bed, and just wept. I cried until I could not cry anymore, then I got up to eat.

That time alone with God grieving was probably a lifesaver. I was able to talk to God about everything that I could think or feel. I gave it all to Him that day. My therapist had also advised me that she was concerned that I would break down under the pressure that I was carrying, and she didn't want that to happen. I believed her based on her knowledge and experience, so I thought it was wisdom to follow her godly, wise counsel. Actually, the ministry staff and those close to me were relieved that I had taken time to care for myself. One friend shared that it was "painful" to watch me in this season of my life carry so much responsibility.

RELATIONSHIPS CHANGED

I felt that my husband had given his all to people at the expense of his own life. Countless days I watched him on the phone counseling during so-called "off hours." He had standing appointments to mentor people, even when I didn't think I could get the time I needed. He had connected to city leaders and projects, etc. He seemed to be there for everyone when they called, needed his counsel, or were experiencing relational problems. Now, the shoe was on the other foot. It felt like Jesus after being captured by the Jewish leaders in the garden; the Scriptures say that all the disciples scattered. I think in many ways, people didn't know how to respond. Therefore, I was shocked when the lady had assumed I didn't need help because help was actually scarce.

Although my husband had survived, this aspect of our lives also felt like a death. Our home that had once been filled with times of fellowship was ghostly silent. The kids lived in their corners of the house when they were home. I guess everyone was doing their best to cope in their own private ways. Sometimes it was difficult for me to be with a couple because it was another reminder of what I had lost. Getting the wheelchair in and out of the vehicle to attend to my husband when we are out fellowshipping is huge.

It feels strange, like a person has passed and you are forced to go on with your life. Everyone has gone on, and you almost feel forgotten even though when you see people, they are quick to say they are still praying. Prayer is good, but it doesn't replace relationship, a call, a card, a meal, or a visit.

WHAT DO YOU DO WITH THE SHAME?

At some point, I realized that I was also dealing with shame or embarrassment when we were out in public, and he would get stares from people. Most people don't know him, but it's the reaction people have to someone in a wheelchair. We still get the looks to this day. Some people may try to help in some small way; others will just let the door slam in your face. It's interesting, to say the least. You can almost hear their thoughts, *What happened to him?* A feeling will come over me to where I want to get him seated as quickly as possible so as to avoid what I am experiencing that no one knows.

Other times, my husband points at people in the restaurant that I don't know, and it's uncomfortable for me. I think in those moments I just want to be invisible. Once, a guy, whom my husband pointed out, came to our table and gave him a big hug. I didn't know the guy and was hoping he didn't ask me if I knew him. He blessed me when he said to my husband, "I tell people all the time that you are responsible for where I am at today in ministry because you spoke over my life." I found out that he was a local pastor on whose life my husband had obviously had a tremendous impact. That is one example that overshadows the shame of people seeing him in that condition.

We receive a variety of reactions; some people are overjoyed to see him, others may break down in tears because it's their first time seeing him. I guess part of the feeling of shame is because I still don't have the answers about the timing of his recovery. One guy recently was telling me his expectation that Timothy would be farther ahead in his recovery; he was one who couldn't bear to see him. I explained that we are witnessing a miracle that he lived and is able to comprehend at the level he does. It's a matter of perspective. I was there in the beginning.

WHO IS TANYA?

That's a great question. Now that I think about it, in one sense I have lost the joy of my fifties in this trauma; it's been a blur in many ways. I am approaching sixty in a couple of years. In some ways, I am still the same at my core; my mindset about being a champion still resides within me. No matter how ironic it seems, that's still my M.O. The champion mentality has carried me through life's toughest challenges. No matter how my life looks now, isn't this what champions are made for?

There were things that I wouldn't have stepped out and achieved previously because as one minister said, "You have been hiding behind your husband." Well, I have been thrust into leadership in a way I never imagined. I can no longer hide or shrink back from the heat of the front lines. I have determined to "fully" embrace all that God has for me. It's this determination that fuels me daily.

As for the woman in me, she is being cared for and nurtured by God; He is truly my sufficiency. The Apostle Paul wrote about his thorn in 2 Corinthians 12:8-9. Jesus gave him a revelation that He wasn't going to remove the thing that tormented Paul. It served a purpose in keeping Paul humble because of the abundance of revelation he had received. Paul became acquainted with the sufficiency of grace. This is when Paul had his "aha" moment and recognized that it was better to have God's supernatural grace and power rest upon him like a tent than to have the thorn removed. I have learned to depend on this same grace; it is indeed supernatural. It's hard to articulate the details of how it works, but it can be clearly seen as I make it through each day.

The mother in me still attempts to guide my children by my example of love for Christ and family. I have always desired to model what I wanted them to become. My daughter still calls me champ when she texts me; that brings me joy because she lives with me and sees everything. I encourage my children to still spend time with their dad for his benefit and theirs. I tell them he's alive, and they can still get love, support, a listening ear, a hug, a proud look, a nod of affirmation, and even an "amen" of approval in their decisions that only a dad can provide.

I have been stretched in so many ways that, in hindsight, I know were necessary to manifest my full potential, but I would like to have changed on my own terms. Trauma has taught me so many lessons about myself, people, life, and God. It's like you gain something that you never could have had if you had not suffered to such a degree. I actually value the transformation because I am not the same person, and I look forward to the opportunities this will afford me in the years to come.

You can still call me a dreamer if you want, but I plan to drink lemonade instead of sucking on lemons.

WHO ARE TIMOTHY AND TANYA?

Although everything has changed, the roles have shifted in every way, and I've assumed the role of caregiver, we have found ways to navigate around and through the difficulties. People often ask me, "How are you able to communicate?" because of Timothy's lack of speech. I explain that I know him so well that I pretty much know everything he would need or want, and the other things I figure out as he dramatizes his request. It is amazing to watch him in action. Recently, he wanted to know how surgery had turned out for one of our faithful members. I had no idea what he was trying to ask. He then laid back on the sofa, and in that moment, I guessed that he was inquiring about the person's surgery who was in the hospital.

   I try my hardest to recover as much of his life as possible, like taking him to ball games that he truly enjoys. I actually now will sit down and enjoy watching more sports on television with him than I did in the past. We have a lot of laughter; that has always been a highlight of our relationship from its inception. He still acts spoiled, as I would call him in times past. For instance, I recently went on a trip to celebrate my forty-year high school class reunion. I took the trip alone, so I could also rest because we had just returned from vacation. As I was packing, he got in bed and indicated that he wanted to be tucked in (I had started doing that after the stroke when he got in bed early enough). It was so cute, and I said, "Aww, the baby wants to be tucked in." Those are just priceless moments of true relationship. I played along with him and laughed and called him spoiled. He loved every moment and went to sleep as I continued to pack.

He called me one hour prior to my arrival via train to check on me. I told him I would be home in an hour. My daughter picked me up and told me that he said to her, "Sugar," which is the new name he gave me. She knew he wanted to make sure she picked me up on time. He was so happy to see me. When my children were in college, it would bring me great joy when they told me he had called to check on them. They would immediately give him an update on their lives. That's still communication. They knew that he cared.

Although everything has changed, the core of our relationship—Timothy and Tanya, the soul mates—is still very much alive and well. When I minister and come down from the stage to my seat, he will either give me a nod of approval, wrap his arm around my shoulder, or just say, "Wow." That in and of itself is strength to me and a great source of joy to know that he thinks I am doing a good job. I value his opinion, especially when it comes to preaching the Word. He is becoming progressively aware of how the ministry is going, and that seems to give him peace.

86 THE DAY My Life Changed

> *Although everything has changed, the core of our relationship—Timothy and Tanya, the soul mates—is still very much alive and well.*

You won't believe this (because I didn't), but today he asked me to cook dressing which is his favorite meal. He literally said, "dressing" for the first time. It's his birthday week, and he is very excited about it. I gathered that he wanted that for his birthday, and he confirmed it. He also heard me on the phone talking to a friend, and they greeted him. He was smiling and said, "Birthday." We all laughed. I don't have to guess what's on his mind; he's now, little by little, getting it out one word at a time, and I'm elated.

CHAPTER SEVEN

The Children's Perspectives

I decided to include our children in this book to describe from their own hearts how their dad's stroke affected their lives. Their perspective should offer additional insight into the overall impact on our family. You will hear from them from eldest to youngest.

BRENDON FORD STOKES

Before my father's stroke, tragedy was something I experienced from a distance. A contained explosion that played out on a stage or movie screen. A fantasy real enough to draw emotion, but safely enjoyed out of harm's way. On March 13, the fantasy ended, and I came face to face with a nightmare I didn't know existed.

The day of my dad's stroke really felt like any other day. I can't exactly remember what I was doing before the accident—a detail that I've misplaced over the years. I do know I was home most of the day. My schedule was clear. It was the kind of day that felt free. No rush to complete any particular task. As I look back the day had a lightness to it. The anticipation of the weekend overshadowed any baggage picked up during the week.

I heard the news from my bedroom or maybe it was the living room—another detail misplaced. What I can recall is my mom shouting to my sister to call an intercessor at our church and tell her to pray. She said, "I think your dad is sick; the ambulance is on its way." Hearing this, shot fear down my spine. I immediately rose to inquire further. I couldn't tell you exactly what message was relayed, but I knew something serious was happening. My immediate reaction was to control what I could control and try to make the transition from our home to the hospital as seamless as possible.

I remember first going to the front door and opening it. I then propped the screen door open to ensure whoever was on the way would be able to enter as quickly as possible. I waited by the door for several minutes, anxiously pacing. It felt like help took forever to arrive. At the sight of the ambulance, I ran down our driveway and waved them in. I remember there being two men who exited the truck. One short and stocky, the other tall and skinny—both too calm in light of the situation at hand. I led them into our home and directed them upstairs to where my dad was.

Up to this point, I hadn't actually seen my father. I only knew what my mother relayed. I did not follow the paramedics into my parents' room. A part of me wasn't ready to face the tragedy. As they worked on my father upstairs, I continued to prepare to make the transition from home to hospital. I started by grabbing the car keys to ensure I'd be ready to drive when the time came. My book bag was conveniently by the door. I had a feeling we would be at the hospital for a while, so it might be helpful to grab snacks and water. I ran to the kitchen to wrangle what sustenance I could. I made it back to the front door with a backpack full of bottled water and a bag of apples. Looking back, it seems silly. What use would a bag of apples do? At the time, though, it was the best idea I could come up with.

After a few minutes, I heard a commotion upstairs. I moved closer to the stairwell and was met with a sight that I can only describe as tragic. The paramedics were carrying my father's limp body down the stairs.

The stocky paramedic had his arms linked under my dad's arms and wrapped around his chest. The skinny one awkwardly hugged his leg. They both seemed to not have a great grip. I remember wanting to step in and lift my father as I imagined he had done for me so many times before. Some things fade away with time; others stick with you. The visual of them carrying my dad down the stairs and out the door to the ambulance is something that I will never forget.

The rest of the story is a blur. Details fade in and out. At the hospital, I was the one who reached out to some of the key people in our life who hadn't heard the news. I remember my first call being to my brother. I quickly relayed to him what I knew, which wasn't much. Dad is sick; we don't know what happened, but we think it's a stroke. I repeated this script several times to friends and family over the phone. I remember breaking down in an empty hospital hallway days later after finding out my father would likely be paralyzed, unable to operate the right side of his body. I remember waiting rooms, vitals, monitors, and trips to the nursing home. I remember my sister being a rock.

I've also forgotten so many details from that day and the days/week/months to follow, but something I've never forgotten is how it felt. In the fantasies I'd observed, tragedy was a momentary speedbump that helped move the plot forward. Something that in the end, made the main character stronger, wiser, and more resilient. Before my father's stroke, I naively thought tragedy would play out the same way in my life—that I would be able to use the bad things that happened to me as fuel to get better and overcome.

What I didn't understand is that what makes a tragic situation so jarring is that no one sees it coming. At one moment you're going about your weekend aimless and free, and the next you're swept into a nightmare you didn't know was possible. After the dust settles, you're left broken, shattered. I've learned a lot from my father's stroke. A lot about that day sticks with me. One thing that I've learned that's carried on is that strength is not always excelling in the face of impossible odds; sometimes strength is picking up the pieces and choosing to make it one more day.

AMBER NICOLE STOKES

The last memory I have of my dad before his stroke is of us eating breakfast together at our favorite diner. I don't remember our conversation, but I remember our window booth, the sun that poured in brightly, turning my dad's hazelnut eyes to honey, the fly that kept buzzing around us, seemingly listening to the ease with which we spoke to each other. We had our own vocabulary, a familiarity we'd built over the past two decades of my life. With each bite of breakfast, I realized there's nothing like having my dad's attention.

There's nothing like having him look at you feeling like he could see every part of you, even the parts you've forgotten or find ugly, and him still staring with no affection spared. It was easy to understand why so many people followed him at our church. Why so many people wanted to call him father. Why so many people held on to his every word. There was nothing like listening to him speak, nothing like listening to his stories, even the stories I knew by heart. Each time he told a story felt like the first time. His words were his magic. Toward the end of breakfast, I remember he told me I was beautiful, and I felt like I was the only girl alive.

There was nothing like listening to him speak, nothing like listening to his stories, even the stories I knew by heart. Each time he told a story felt like the first time. His words were his magic.

Before March 13, 2015, I had never seen my dad sick. I watched him toss my brothers over each shoulder; I saw him bench press 250 pounds; I witnessed him bring a crowd of a thousand churchgoers to their feet, but I'd never seen him sick. So to see food spilling out of his mouth and onto his pillowcase, urine soaking the sheets, and eyes glossy, unseeing, and hollow are images my body will never be able to process. And yet I remember standing over him trying to do just that. I remember my mom told me to get a towel to clean the vomit, and I couldn't do it. I remember my mom telling me to get his ID for the first responders. I couldn't do it. I remember trying to get him to see me: "Look at me, Dad." And thinking, *Why can't he look at me?* He couldn't do it.

We started praying for miracles in the hospital. My faith was stronger then, partly because I was closer to God (when you are in a crisis, God feels like He's right there with you pacing the vinyl floors). And partly because, at the time, I thought he had a temporary illness. Since the memory of my dad before his stroke was so close, I couldn't imagine losing that forever. Now, nearly eight years later, I can't imagine getting him back. And what do we mean when we pray for full recovery or wish for him to "come back"? I have no answer for this. I wonder if we all think this is just an understudy playing my dad—a second best to fill in only when the original is sick. We as people have a hard time letting both versions share the same stage. Can we not accept him for selfish reasons? Is this hope that he'll get better keeping us alive? Praying for miracles has made me extremely discontent because it makes it hard to love the dad I have now—hard to accept the dad I have now. Praying for miracles feels like we are saying, "I love you but not enough to accept you the way you are now, not enough to take care of you the way you are now." The girl who believed in the miracles she prayed for is still in the hospital outside of the ER, nineteen, big-eyed, holding onto a twenty-pound Bible, and desperate.

Today he said, "Birthday." Today he said, "Blessed." Today he said, "Basketball, burger, movies." "Today he said your name." These are all updates my mom will excitedly tell me with her eyes full of shock and hope. But each new word he says just makes me grieve all the words he can't say. I can't hear him say, "I'm proud of you," "You're a trip, Dubers," "Let the church say amen," or even "You are beautiful." Am I grieving the loss of his magic? I'm not sure, because I still see it. Sometimes it's just a look; other times it's the way he'll call me in the room to give me a hug just because we haven't hugged in a while. The way he makes funny faces behind my mom's back when she's nagging at us. The way he still thinks I'm funny. The way I still think he's hilarious. It's in the way he's attentive (or rather, nosey). In the way he keeps up with me and somehow still knows about every detail of my life.

A lot of time has passed. Our favorite diner is closed now. And I believe the miracle is something we've already seen—the miracle of God keeping my dad alive. My dad did come back. I believe that. The miracle is that anytime I want, I can see my dad and kiss his cheek; when I hug him, I can feel him holding me tight. I can make him laugh at a silly joke; we can cheer for our favorite basketball team together. And no, he can't say every word, but we still have our own vocabulary. He's still here. But I'm greedy. And I want one last story. I want more magic. I want to feel alive again.

EMMANUEL COLE STOKES

Growing up, all I knew was growth. The exciting growth of a ministry, which came with financial growth and a new home fit for royalty. The growth of family and friends, the growth of the knowledge of God and His plans for this earth. And at the forefront of all this growth was my father (along with my mother, of course). He grew to be one of the most influential people in the city of Flint. He was the coolest man I knew; he was Superman, and my life felt complete. But quickly, my good thing came to an end.

When the housing market crashed, many members—some of whom were my friends—left the church and relocated in search of financial stability. Following that, the church was hit with an array of trials, internally and externally. Then the final blow came. In March of 2015, I got a call while at a high school basketball game. My sister was on the line, telling me that dad had had a stroke and that he was in the ER of Hurley Hospital, fighting for his life. As I stood in disbelief, I wondered how something so destructive could be so blindsiding, how a behemoth could attack in silence. Just thirty seconds ago my mind was at peace, and now, all of a sudden, I've lost touch with reality.

How does losing a father's guidance affect one's moral compass, or seeing your hero fall affect one's courage? How does a natural tragedy affect a spiritual family? Before any of these questions could be answered, I was on a plane with my father southbound to Arizona, which presented a new, more pressing question: How does being your father's primary caretaker for

THE CHILDREN'S PERSPECTIVES 95

two months in a foreign location shape one's mind? But first, I want to tell you how I ended up on that plane.

Once my dad was healthy enough to start some additional rehab therapy, my mother pulled some strings, like the hard-working administrator she is, and found a really good physical therapist in Tucson, Arizona, who wasn't too far away from her old high school friend in Gilbert. So, one thing led to another, and we figured out that we could have my dad do this therapy for a couple months. Only one question remained unanswered: "Who's going to go down to Arizona for two months with him?"

The decision was quite easy. My younger brother was too young. My sister was, well, a girl. My older brother had a job and other responsibilities, and the same was true of my mother. She had a church to run and mouths to feed. So that left Yours Truly. I had no present responsibilities, and I was eighteen, so in June of 2016, off I went.

To say that this was a big adjustment for me would be an understatement. The weather was hotter than a demon with halitosis, I had to learn how to cook and be all-around responsible, and most challenging of all, I felt alone and broken while being asked to be there for my dad and help repair him. It's interesting what different circumstances will bring out of you when you don't have a choice but to move forward. As I write this, I'm realizing that despite no longer having the guidance of a father, I still learned a valuable lesson in manhood: duty.

> *It's interesting what different circumstances will bring out of you when you don't have a choice but to move forward.*

I see now that, as a man with responsibilities, the whole world could fall on your shoulders, and you're expected to carry it. That despite your feelings, you have to be a rock, a go-to, a provider, and I learned how to be that in Arizona. I experienced a lot of pain down there which turned out to be growth, and I'm grateful I was able to be there for my father. He got a lot stronger, and it built a great foundation for further growth back at home.

If you're wondering how I'm handling this domestic conundrum today in 2022, it's hard to say. I feel like I'm living a contradicting life, strolling through limbo. The father I knew is no longer here, but I still have a father. How do you miss someone that's still alive? I'm realizing that sometimes in life there are no answers, just options: love or don't love. I'm choosing the former, of course. So yeah, I'm no longer traumatized, but I'm definitely still healing.

As I'm adjusting to this new normal, I'm able to find some silver linings with my dad. I see that even though he is different, he still has his charm along with his same sense of humor. Also, he seems to be at peace, content with just being, which definitely helps me handle his condition stress-free.

And even though he can't speak to me and guide me like he did before, I hear his past words of wisdom loud and clear, and now I cherish them like a family heirloom. Also, through this journey, I've actually gotten to know my dad better from people's testimonials of him. I'm continually shocked by how many people my dad impacted throughout his life. I've heard so many stories of his profound nature, and it pushes me to become the greatest I can be. To become Superman.

So yeah, this journey has been anything but easy, and I still miss my father so much it breaks my heart, but I'm learning that this is what they call life. Nothing is promised, and nothing is forever, so hug your loved ones today and tell them how much they mean to you.

I love you, Dad.

TIMOTHY RAY STOKES II

I had heard that when someone has a traumatic experience they remember every detail, but until I experienced it myself, I could not appreciate the accuracy of that statement. While the memory of my father's voice has left me, I don't think I will ever forget the face I saw while he was having his stroke.

On March 13, 2015, a 13-year-old boy would experience such a loss that he would not understand the depths of it even until the time of his writing about it seven years later. I came home from school on Friday, excited to finish my homework and begin playing a videogame, as I could only play on weekends. I had to write a paper first, so I went into my parent's room to grab my mother's computer and saw my father taking a nap.

Distinctly remembering how adamant he was against naps, I was taken aback but continued my quest to finish homework.

Once the paper was done, I returned the computer and was again surprised by my father napping. This time however, I found it even more strange because he seemed to be lifting one arm up and trying to wake up. Maybe, if I'd realized what was going on, this story would be different. I was only thirteen at the time though; how could I have known it was a stroke? I proceeded out of the room suppressing my urge to comment on what I believed to be hypocritical behavior—my father, so adamant against naps, taking one himself. Unbelievable. Unfortunately ignorant, I continued on to play my game.

After a considerable amount of time playing, I was interrupted by my sister, Amber, who said, "Get ready, we need to go to the hospital. Dad is nonresponsive." My young head could not comprehend the severity of that statement, so I nonchalantly gathered my things and got ready to go.

Upon arriving at the hospital, my siblings and I would spend the night surrounded by friends and family. They told me my father had a stroke, so of course I looked online to see what it meant. "Oh, it could be fatal," I thought as worry began to settle in. This was no longer the minor issue I had perceived it to be, and at the time I don't think there was any way I could have realized just how much it would affect me.

Hoping to have some semblance of normalcy in my life, I fought to go to my school auction the following day, while my father was still in critical condition. Perhaps this was the start of what would be a grandiose ignoring of feelings and compartmentalization of emotion for me, but who knows?

My eldest brother, in an act of wisdom, had agreed to let me go on the condition that I journaled my feelings regularly. Unfortunately, one party—me—reneged on the deal, perhaps contributing to what would become years of emotional escapism.

Nonetheless, I went to the auction and had fun. However, I would eventually return to the hospital and in the words of Eminem, "Snap back to reality," and a hard reality this was. A day in the hospital turned into a week, turned into a month, turned into six months; like a slow, lethal poison reality setting in, crippling the hope of a return to normalcy.

During the height of my adolescence, as a now fourteen-year-old boy, I would have to face the cold reality that life would never be the same. Ill-equipped for the fight, I retreated behind a wall of good grades, charisma, anime, and other empty pursuits without realizing that ignoring my problems and feelings would only cause even greater pain in the future. I was ignorant. How could I know? How do I figure out how I feel? That's a question I still struggle with today as a twenty-one-year-old man. So how, as a fourteen-year-old, could I have found that answer? I do not know if I could have, and I have long since ceased wondering about the hypotheticals.

Throughout my life, I have seen the effects of losing my dad manifest in different ways. Although my dad survived, our relationship has changed dramatically with his inability to speak. I've mourned the loss of my father, learning how to grieve in specific ways. I grieved that I lost the father figure who would teach me how to treat women in a relationship... that I lost the man who should show me how to be a strong man that

100 THE DAY *My Life Changed*

is sensitive to those around him . . . that I lost my golf rival . . . and that I lost an extremely wise spiritual figure.

I have learned to compartmentalize in a new, healthier way, slowly understanding just how much I've lost and, one step at a time, grieving such loss. There is so much I wish I could have told that thirteen-year-old boy—so much he needed to know to prepare him for March 13, 2015. He did not realize that his life would never be the same, but if I could tell him only one thing, knowing where he'd end up, I'd say with a smile, "You're gonna be just fine, kid."

Front row from left to right: Michelle Hill, Gail Freeman, Tanya, Timothy II, Amber
Second row from left to right: Mary Hood, Emmanuel Stokes, Brendon Stokes

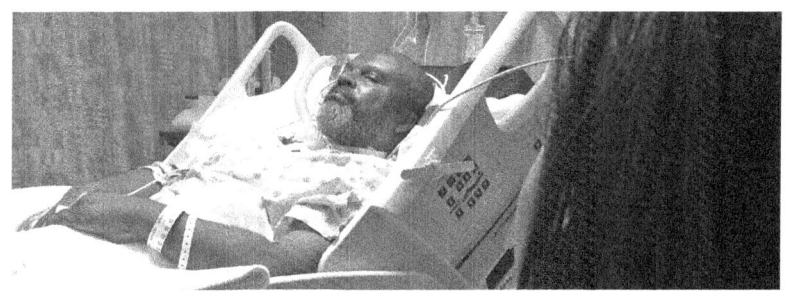

Amber visiting her dad in ICU

Timothy relaxing at home while Amber looks on

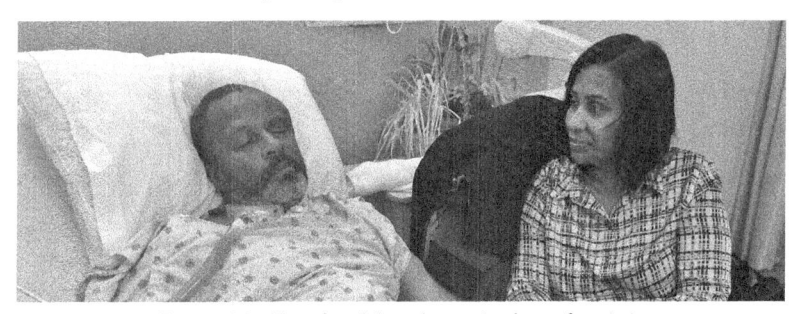

Tanya visiting Timothy while at the nursing home for rehab

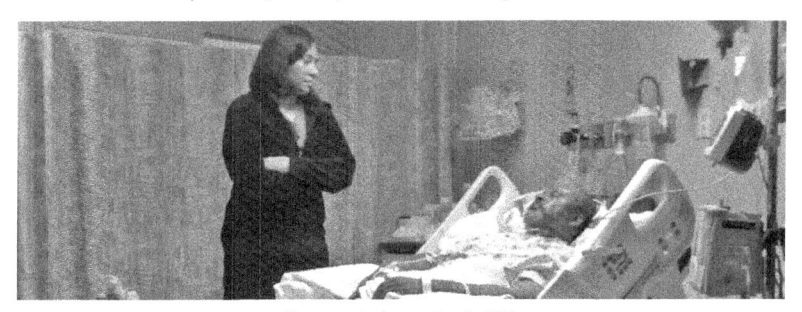

Tanya quietly praying in ICU

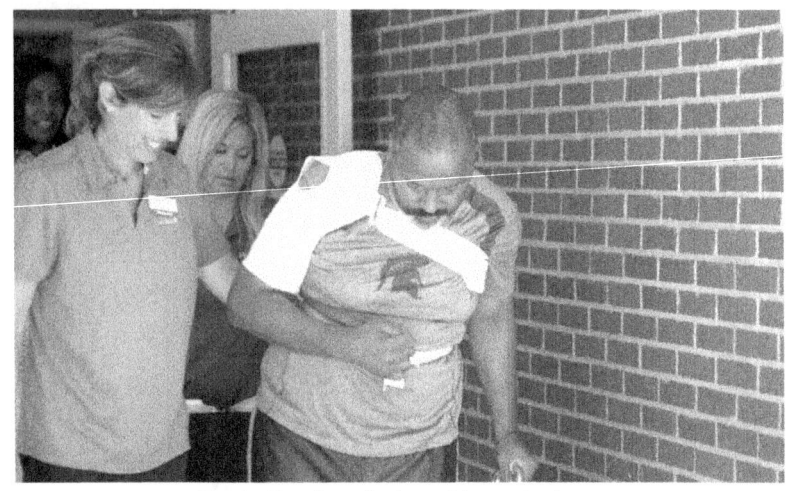

The day Timothy walked out of the nursing home

The day Timothy walked out of the nursing home

CHAPTER EIGHT

Picking Up the Shattered Pieces

WHO IS TANYA NOW?

The question now is, "Who is Tanya?" The second T in TNT. Change is inevitable; as the song says, "Everything must change. Nothing and no one remains the same." I agree, but forced change is invasive, without sensitivity, and numb to the pain and angst it causes. You literally have to change to survive change. As I sorted through the rubbish after the storm in an attempt to salvage something that resembled the life I once knew so well, I didn't find a single area that escaped the need to be refurbished. I had to rebuild my entire life.

I had to rebuild my entire life.

"Who is Tanya?" This was the question my mentor, Dr. David Ireland, asked me as he coached me to take the helm of the ministry that my husband and I had built together. My response to Dr. Ireland was an explanation of how I had never seen myself in the lead role before. His reply was, "That was then; who is Tanya now?" I could clearly see the changed woman was glaring back at me as I, in a flash of my imagination, revisited the woman whom I once knew. I quickly responded, "You're right. I'm not the same woman that I was six months ago." Embracing his counsel and the counsel of other spiritual leaders, I said yes to the assignment. Besides, at the age of twelve, on my knees in prayer, I vividly recall promising God that I would do "whatever He wanted me to do," with no idea of the roads those words would cause me to tread even now alone.

Even though I knew I was different, it didn't stop the struggle within to rise to the new demands that were on my life, in the midst of still caring for my husband. What I had never envisioned was the T without the other T. We had worked so long together and so well that I felt we were better together. Prior to the stroke, thoughts of me branching out doing things on my own seemed foreign and kept me from pursuing things that were on my heart, as I vacillated between the feeling of not being teammates in the project. Perhaps, I was hiding behind underlying fear of branching out on my own. I am convinced that I'm a natural-born leader. No person or circumstance can take that from me. But within, I was still contemplating that question, "Have my proven trophies in sports and various leadership roles adequately prepared me for this role?" These questions plagued me as I met new challenges seemingly daily. Who is Tanya? I had hidden behind my husband for years. One guest minister at our church called me out on that fact. When I thought about it, I agreed that I had taken a "behind him" role at times. It wasn't hard to stand beside my husband in support of him since he oozed with confidence in everything. Even when faced with new challenges, he figured things out and still moved forward with assurance. That was his M.O.

Ministry is different from athletic achievements in that it's not a game. You deal with real people with real problems. You need to have skills in multiple areas. I think with my husband's level of skill in the Word of God, it was easy to feel unqualified or that I didn't know enough. Ministry is lifelong learning, so even after having obtained a Master's Degree in Theology, I still didn't feel as if I knew enough.

THE SHIFT

A pivotal point in me moving forward "without" my husband came when I chose to graduate without him. We had decided to attend school together and to graduate together. There was a period of time when we stopped going because the church was growing and the demands were increasing beyond our ability to manage both. I didn't want to stop because I'm a finisher, but he insisted we wait until a better time, so I conceded. The college offered tuition at half price for the spouse, so it was beneficial for us to attend together.

Before long, years had passed and still no degree. Then I ended up pregnant (unexpectedly) with our youngest son,

Timothy. My husband again insisted that I wait until Timothy was school age before returning to school—that ended up being another six to seven years. Plus, the degree required ninety-six credits and we may have only had a third of those completed. We finally re-enrolled because of my determination to finish. The stroke occurred on the final leg of that journey. The paper that I was literally writing at the time of the stroke was "How to be led by the Holy Spirit."

I decided that I was going to finish the paper after my husband had gotten placed in the nursing home. So, at night after I returned home, I wrote. Although I had finished my paper, I still decided I wasn't going to attend my graduation. I called the school and found out that if I didn't walk in 2015, I could still walk in 2016, but not thereafter. It was April, and I was at the nursing home when I felt a gentle nudge within that said, *Call the school and see if you can still walk.* I called and found out that it wasn't too late, so I had them order my cap and gown and decided it was best for me to do it ALONE.

This was HUGE. Timothy and I had worked all those years together to finish together, and I would have to walk alone. That was another "moment" of change that I was forced to embrace to enter into my own future. With my husband at the nursing home and not able to attend my graduation, it was a bittersweet victory. For Tanya to have finished her goal after years of holding on to it, having to walk alone was unimaginable. I had a slightly guilty feeling for walking without him because of our commitment to walk together. Nonetheless, the budding of the new Tanya was seen in every step across that stage. It meant more than achieving a goal; it was the re-emergence of a relentless champion with whom I once was well acquainted. In my experience, there's nothing that will shake your self-confidence like being a servant of God. Who can feel self-confident before an all-knowing, all-seeing, all-powerful God? The Apostle Paul was arguably the greatest apostle. Yet, he understood that his sufficiency wasn't in himself but in God alone. Paul stated, "Not that we are sufficient of ourselves to think anything as of ourselves; but our sufficiency is of God" (2 Corinthians 3:5, KJV).

There's a time for teamwork, but sometimes you must go it alone. This was foreign to me as a wife. I never realized how much of my life was connected to my husband's—literally every decision that I made was in consideration of him. But that's what I had learned that I signed up for. God commanded the husband in the beginning of time, "Therefore shall a man leave his father and his mother; and shall cleave unto his wife: and they shall be one flesh" (Genesis 2:24, KJV). I saw myself as the "helper suitable for him" by God's design (Genesis 2:18, NIV).

In many ways, Tanya had taken a back seat to push him forward. I was capable and comfortable in that role. I felt enough of the darts thrown at me just being his wife: the criticism, the cruel remarks by the misinformed, the misunderstanding of who you are, the judgment. As a wife, I hurt for him and had to bear my own cross from the critics who hide in obscurity and throw rocks at those out front. My perspective at that time was that I most certainly carried enough of a load just walking beside him; that was enough of a cross for me to bear.

When I returned to the nursing home that evening after graduation and showed him the photos, I think he did the best he could to convey that he was happy for me. I am certain it was bittersweet. Even his mom had shown, for the first time, what I saw as a distinction between me (the daughter-in-law) and her son. She attended the graduation but couldn't help but desire for her son to be there as well. She even grabbed a mug they were giving the graduates to take to my husband. I almost felt like that was her greatest concern. I didn't hold that against her. I couldn't imagine what she was feeling for her son, who was her pride and joy, who wasn't able to share in this moment that he had worked for as well. Needless to say, I fought through all of those emotions to step into a moment that I had to embrace, being true to Tanya. It was time for Tanya to arise, totally outside of my comfort zone, as I was rediscovering who I was, independent from Timothy.

FAMILY IN THE AFTERMATH

It took time for me to see the devastation in my family, perhaps because of my focus on my husband's recovery. My children will open up every now and then to speak of their pain and the impact of their "loss," especially at a critical time in their lives. I think in other ways, they have "acted out" their loss by being aloof.

Recently, on the Fourth of July holiday when we were sharing a family moment, I spoke about some things that I shared in the book. My daughter finally spoke up and asked me to share it at another time because they were reliving the event as I spoke. My two other sons who were present chimed in and said it was a downer. I apologized because I didn't know it would affect them that way, and we shifted the conversation to save the day of fun and fellowship. We just don't really "go there" any longer. I see that the pain runs deep in them as well for good reasons; they all speak of their dad as their hero. I've carried the burden of yet rebuilding a close-knit family again.

The damage is deep. The pain still lies under the surface, most often too deep for words. The struggle for me is to guide three young men when I know that "It takes a man to raise a man," according to my mentor Dr. Ireland. I have even had to rely on my spiritual father, Dr. Phillip Goudeaux, and other men of God to counsel my sons. *Lord, give me wisdom to parent them in this season,* is my continual prayer.

Little by little, we are rebuilding. It's paradoxical how a trial can turn to triumph, how weakness becomes strength, how sorrow turns to joy, but it does indeed. All of these seemingly small victories bleed through to soothe the unspoken pain that seems to want to take up permanent residence. I consider this trial another trophy for God's glory. That is the impetus for my hope!

LIFE WITHOUT HIS VOICE

You may wonder what the hardest part of my journey is. Hands down, I would have to say it's the loss of Timothy's speech. Words of affirmation rank high on my love language list. Imagine the impact of silence. I often go back and read the last words he wrote about me at a Valentine's Day event a couple weeks prior to when our world went silent.

There was also something huge that had transpired the year before when I turned fifty. I decided to celebrate for fifty days, so he was inspired to write me a poem for each day. I have his words displayed in a large frame to revisit when I need to hear his voice. Although he was a poet, he had rarely written *me* poetry. I think his mentality was that of his dad's, *I have you now*. But I wanted the poetry like he had formerly written others whom he had dated prior to our meeting. He had told me all about the stories. To my surprise, every day of the fifty-day celebration he granted me the best gift ever: the words from his heart concerning me. This was a treasure then, but it's priceless now. I never want to lose that.

It has been amazing to see how this "master communicator" has navigated around speech. It's as if we are playing the game of charades. I generally am able to figure out what he is trying to say. That remnant blesses me beyond measure because it eases both of our frustration: his when I don't get it, mine when I don't get it. Those are also moments when grace bleeds through and we can keep it moving, regardless of the mountain of a barrier. There have been times when he communicated to people that we were going on vacation and other things that they questioned me about after communicating with him. I was amazed that he was able to give them the 411, so to speak. Hope leaps once again in those scenarios.

Sometimes I visit his old preached messages to hear his voice or call his cellphone which still has his voice recorded. I say to myself, *Yes, that's the voice that I remember. That's the highly treasured voice that even the people of God are awaiting.* I called one of our church members on her birthday and left a message with my husband singing happy birthday. She returned the call totally broken down in tears and joy that I did that for her; that's a small indication of what his voice means to us all. To one of our senior leaders, Timothy's voice was so important that the leader visited him in the nursing home, so my husband could pray for him (even though Timothy didn't have a voice).

I think everyone would just be happy to hear his voice again as they were when I surprised them and had him sing in the mic the happy birthday song to all those celebrating that month. Usually, the worship leader would sing. The church was ecstatic; some even cried as they had longed to just hear his voice once again. His voice has become even more precious than before. As the famous saying goes, "You don't miss your water until your well runs dry."

TURNING LEMONS INTO LEMONADE

What would I give to have our lives back? Everything to have a do-over with the priceless wisdom I have gained. But, there is a saying that I believe in: "Turning lemons into lemonade." Those are not just empty words; I am certain they were birthed in adversity. How do sour, real-life circumstances become sweet? Is this really a possibility or a fantasy? I believe it's a matter of perspective—whether you look at the glass as being half empty or half full. I choose to see it as half full. I am an optimist at my core, believing that "there is a way."

As I said earlier, the great apostle Paul saw his trial as an opportunity, an opportunity to experience more of Christ's power and ability which required human weakness. Both weakness and strength were occurring simultaneously as

Paul's weakness encountered Jesus's strength. The grace that Jesus offered was a place of power that depends on weakness to draw it out. Admittedly, I am weak. We are weak. In our weakness, we receive His strength that is able to sustain us no matter the outcome of the circumstance. That's my focus.

Paul's outlook was to seize that opportunity of receiving supernatural empowerment rather than being freed from the trial. What he would learn and experience from Christ would be far greater than the discomfort of the thorn. The key is the admission of human weakness, which is the challenge in our prideful western culture. I have discovered that ministry is also an environment where people feel as if they have to appear to be strong, even if they aren't, to save spiritual face. Not only that, it is challenging to find people whom you can trust with your delicate stuff. Paul had it right: Say what you want to say about why I am in the situation; I am going to focus on the opportunity it affords me to boast in the Lord. God is ultimately going to get the glory out of my life.

One of the things that I desired to do, even just months prior to the stroke, was to birth a television program. It was tough getting in front of a camera for the first time in years. Things were foggy; I had no clear vision of the purpose I had once known as my destiny. Last year, I birthed my television show with the greatest clarity ever. Six years of growth from my trial had given me a message. I learned and grew as I launched into the deep. It was amazing to see Tanya again, the Tanya who had been told by a college professor, "You can go as far as you want to in television media because of your camera presence and ability." I launched it, even in my uncertainty, fear, and concern as to whether I was still good enough and all the other nuances that come with that territory. This is an example of turning lemons into lemonade.

I have also developed leadership classes that have been in my heart for years. I am writing again, which I haven't done in years. There are many other projects that I am working on developing to meet the needs of people.

There is a song that says, "Ain't He good. Ain't He real good." Although it's not good English (on purpose), we get our praise on at church by singing this song as we proclaim the goodness of God. To be able to praise the Lord in the midst of trial, drinking of His sweetness while tasting His goodness, is to live! My conversation with God is, "As long as You don't leave me, I'm good. We are going to be alright." I know that He promised that He would never leave nor forsake His children. The lemonade is sweet. Life is good because God is good.

The lemonade is sweet. Life is good because God is good.

CHAPTER NINE
I'm Hopeful

THE ROLE OF HOPE IN TRAUMA

You may not be able to control what happens to you, but you can control your response. I choose to believe that the Lord is working things together for my good (Romans 8:28). Early on in this journey, I saw God working in the midst of my calamity. He still provided for our personal needs and the needs of the ministry. I grew in greater dependence on the Lord for everything. There was a core group of people who were determined to stand with us. I have gathered several strategic mentors and leaders who help guide me. I have grown in a variety of ways—in character, in spirit, in leadership capacity, in wisdom, as a parent, and in various other ways.

You may not be able to control what happens to you, but you can control your response.

I refuse to let the devil claim victory in my life! Athletics taught me invaluable lessons on how to allow adversity to make me rather than break me. I admit that I have a very strong will to win. However, a strong will alone isn't the secret to overcoming deep trauma that hits our lives. The secret is a strong God behind the strong will. Again, I have discovered the depth of my weakness and God's inexhaustible strength.

Every day for more than seven years, I have looked at the reality of being hit by a tsunami-strength storm that left obvious devastating damage. At the same time, I believe it's not over and that my husband will fully recover. This is evidence that hope is still alive. My perspective is that God wouldn't have allowed this if a greater good wasn't going to be born. People cannot truly understand what it takes to not only survive but thrive after severe trauma unless it is from their own personal experience. It seems miraculous just to maintain a sound mind, to not drown in your own sorrow, let alone be able to help others and have laughter, even if it's through the occasional tears. These are all benefits of the grace that I described earlier. It is also what keeps hope alive!

The ability to hope enables us to do things like see the light at the end of the tunnel, to envision a brighter day, to anticipate the arrival of spring while in the throes of a brutal winter. I have set myself to hope. There are people who expect the worse whom the world calls pessimistic thinkers. I'm the opposite; I expect the best, even if I have to deal with disappointment if things don't happen as I desire. I choose to believe! I've been serving the Lord since I was twelve, and I have more than forty-six years of relational experience with Him. He has never failed me, and neither will He ever fail you—that is impossible! He is an all-knowing, all-seeing, all-wise, loving God.

When I can't see and understand, God knows what's best. It reminds me of being a parent; my children don't fully understand the things that I share with them to protect them from potential harm. Wisdom is farsighted, and children, who don't have much life experience, can't see that far. At a certain point in my life, I even admitted that my parents were right in their counsel and concerns, even though I thought I knew what was best. They really did know best. The same is true with our relationship with our Creator—I guarantee you He knows best.

ONE DAY AT A TIME

The concept of taking one day at a time may seem obvious. In actuality, today is all we will ever really have. However, when you are a forward thinker who loves to look ahead and plan accordingly, it's a challenge to be fully present in the now. Jesus gave His take on tomorrow in the context of worrying. He advised His followers not to be anxious about tomorrow for the simple fact that each day already has enough problems (Matthew 6:34, KJV).

Living by a plan is a good thing, but one must be cautious as to not carry the burden of tomorrow on his shoulders. I could not look far into the future as I was accustomed to doing. I decided to go with the flow of what today would bring. Besides, it's a challenge to plan ahead. Should I downsize? Where will I live? What support would I need in place to assist me as we age? What other stream of income could I create to help relieve the burden? Will I be able to lead the ministry into its next area of growth and fruitfulness? What additional skills do I need to acquire? I have a ton of questions that require real thoughtfulness. I will seek solutions for all of them but take one day at a time. The saying goes like this: "How do you eat an elephant?" The answer is simple: "One bite at a time."

Living too far ahead mentally and emotionally can definitely be an opportunity for worry to creep in and paralyze you. Major decisions must be well thought-out, prayed out, and accompanied by plenty of godly counsel to ensure you are headed in the right direction. I am forced to live one day at a time.

The key is that I am "living" one day at a time, not merely existing to pass the time. We have always been a couple who lived purposefully, intentionally, and strategically. We aren't going to resort to a life of nothingness by default. We will just face each day thankfully as it arrives with the gratitude one should possess toward God's provision. One day at a time is enough for any of us to face.

FINDING JOY IN SORROW

I am learning that the nature of joy transcends circumstances. You find this concept throughout Scripture where joy was available in spite of circumstances. I don't know if you're familiar with Paul and Silas, who had been imprisoned for preaching the gospel. We are told that they were singing hymns and praises to God at midnight to where all the other prisoners could hear them. Notice, it didn't say they were down and out, depressed, complaining about how they were unjustly treated (Acts 16:16). They had joy. There were other times when the disciples were beaten by the religious authorities for not obeying their command to stop spreading the gospel of Jesus Christ, and they counted it an honor to be considered worthy to be beaten. It's a fallacy to think that Christians won't go through tough times or ever become sick. Jesus let His disciples know upfront, "In this world, you will have trouble." But He also encouraged them to be full of joy, regardless: "Be of good cheer [because] I have overcome the world" (John 16:33, KJV).

Jesus had to endure the cross, but it was joy that was set before Him (Hebrews 12:2). We are told to fix our eyes on Jesus. In other words, He serves as an example for us to emulate as it relates to having joy in suffering. The Apostle James says to count it all joy when you fall into diverse temptations, knowing that the trying of your faith works something within (James 1:2). Trials are designed to build—not kill—a person's faith. It's joy that will get you through the storm. The Holy Spirit is the One who produces the joy in believers by His presence as we yield to His promptings (Galatians 5:22-23). Therefore, the possibility for joy is always present internally, no matter what you experience externally. It is not contingent on your circumstances.

How do you find joy in trauma? In His presence is the fullness of joy; at His right hand there are pleasures evermore (Psalm 16:11). Joy is found in God's presence. God's presence is in every believer. The believer can have joy at any time, in any circumstance. I choose to find joy because it is a benefit of being a citizen in God's kingdom (Romans 14:17).

> *The believer can have joy at any time, in any circumstance. I choose to find joy because it is a benefit of being a citizen in God's kingdom.*

Every morning I awake, I think about God first and not my situation. I thank Him for another day. I meditate on His goodness demonstrated for the entirety of my life. I think about and thank Him for providing for me everything that I need—and then some. Thinking about God always brings me joy. No matter what I have to deal with during the day, my thoughts of God always provide me with exactly what I need whenever I need it. My life in God will not be boxed into natural, seemingly unfavorable circumstances. In everything give thanks for this is the will of God concerning thee (1Thessalonians 5:18). I choose joy.

OVERCOMING FEARS AND DOUBTS

You may wonder whether I have fears or doubts about whether this story will end with the ultimate outcome of total recovery. I can honestly say that there are times when I look at my husband with my natural eyes, and there is a constant reminder of the reality which could have taken me down the road of hopelessness, if I allowed it. This natural reality does seem as if it's impossible to overcome. I know how huge this is from all natural points of view.

In my walk with Christ, I have learned that fears and doubts are always present, demanding expression. It is just a matter of whether you yield to their promptings. Jesus once spoke of how with man, things (specifically salvation) are impossible, but with God all things are possible (Matthew 19:26); that is where I am locked in. Medically speaking, I may be witnessing the best that I can expect. With the God factor, I believe there is nothing too hard for God. The simple fact that my husband is increasingly able to say more words is amazing to me. It feels like a sign of the hope of God's goodness seeping through the frailty of human ability.

Sure, I would love to have a date and time in which the manifestation of my expectation will arrive at my home, but that's not how God works. It is natural for thoughts to enter my mind that would love for me to embrace his current condition as the best that I should expect. Thoughts of fear have tried to paint a picture of the possibility of this being a lifelong sentence, so to speak. These are fleeting thoughts that I am able to overcome by a continual focus on my expectation and God's ability.

HONORING MY SACRED VOWS

On our wedding day, we vowed to remain in our covenant relationship "until death do we part." That was an upfront commitment that we made, not knowing what life together would bring in the days ahead. Many people comment as to how amazed they are that I remained with my husband after the stroke. That wasn't even a decision I had to ponder; it was made for me September 26, 1987, in holy matrimony. I am confident that he would do the same for me had the shoe been on the other foot. Also, as I indicated earlier, our lives were literally joined together in every way. As in the case of Siamese twins, there would have to be some type of miraculous operation to separate us.

I attempt to make his life as enjoyable as possible as a way of preserving his dignity in hopes of causing him to still feel significant in the family. He still has a voice. I may be speaking as if staying and caring for him personally has been easy. Actually, nothing about this journey has been easy, but I feel it's the godly thing to do. I live from a place of being true to my heart. This is where my heart lies. In many ways, the relationship is still intact, even through the dramatic change. He still loves to laugh at a good joke; we enjoy more laughter now than at other times in our relationship.

Yes, we do "get on each other's nerves," the usual, husband and wife kind of stuff. I maintain my respect for him, but he knows when I am serious. For instance, I may go up and down the stairs attending to his needs. When I'm done, I'm done. I will graciously inform him, "That's it, buddy. I am headed to bed." My sister, who was staying with us for a short period of time, felt that I was being insensitive, but I had to stop at some point. Tomorrow is a new day. Besides, after thirty-five years of marriage, he knows me well. When I say I'm done, he knows he has gone past his grace. There's a saying that goes like this: "Different strokes for different folks." It just speaks to the diversity of people, their likes and dislikes. I operate according to our relationship, so things work out just fine for us.

CHAPTER TEN
The Final Say

GOD HAS THE FINAL SAY

Ultimately, as in all things, God has the final say in the matter. As I said earlier, I had to release the burden of Timothy's healing from my shoulders, for I am not a miracle worker. Although his mother passed in October of 2021, she died still believing God would heal him. It actually shocked me to look at a proclamation that she had on her bathroom wall that obviously she would pray over my husband for his healing. That touched my heart deeply that she was still engaged in prayer for him.

I, too, am a firm believer in prayer. I have experienced some amazing answers to prayer that assure me of the fact that God hears our prayers, and He also answers. Of course, I also understand that we don't have a blank check to receive whatever we desire. Scripture is clear that we must pray according to God's will (Matthew 6:9-13, 1 John 5:14). My son, Emmanuel, once asked, as he and I were standing in my kitchen, "Why is it that we can't just accept his condition as it is? Maybe this is the way it is going to be." It is because of my faith in God as a healer, my personal experience in God sparing my life from cancer, and God's delight in answering our prayers that I continue to believe. God has the final answer. I haven't heard no, so I will persist.

God has the final answer.

I am also a dreamer, and I have had too many dreams of his full recovery to throw away my confidence. We recently began posting my husband's sermons on the church's YouTube channel (Family Worship Center Channel). It is encouraging to see the attention they receive. His messages were timeless, so we thought they would still be able to have impact on people's lives in their walk with Christ. That's who we are, servants of Christ who are called and separated unto the gospel. It's in my nature, according to my parents, to not let go of things that I set my mind to do. Without such tenacity, I would not have survived in my marriage, ministry, or in life itself. I think putting my whole life in the arms of God is the best option.

I REFUSE TO NOT BELIEVE

Where do we go from here? My strategy and aim are to keep fighting the good fight of faith. As believers, God requires faith. The entirety of our relationship is based on faith in Him. Scripture teaches us that without faith it is impossible to please Him (Hebrews 11:6). I believe God is still a healer today; His healing power is not confined to the early church days. Jesus is the same yesterday, today, and forever (Hebrews 13:8).

It's interesting to live by faith because physical reality can be so overwhelming. Prior to my trial, there were many days that I just took for granted. Many times, I was so overwhelmed by trials, suffering, and the stress of everyday life that I didn't stop and thank God for the small things like sunshine. I have learned to smell the roses; even a bright sun-shining day now brings me great joy in the midst of sorrow. For that, I am thankful because God always displays signs of His goodness if we are willing to see what He has done and is doing.

I choose to see Him as a good God (Psalm 107:1), who is good all the time. Therefore, when my circumstance isn't good, I still have hope because God is good in the circumstance. The psalmist, King David, invited us to do what he learned to do: "Oh, taste and see that the Lord is good" (Psalm 34:8, ESV). When I want to lament, I taste and see that the Lord is good. When I'm nearing a point of weariness in my journey, I taste and see that the Lord is good. When I want to know when this will come to an end, and I don't get a specific answer, I taste and see that the Lord is good. The Word of God isn't theory to me; I have a living hope that provides me with what I need when I need it.

The second half of the verse David penned in Psalm 34 reads, "blessed is the man who takes refuge in him" (v. 8, ESV). That's the heart of my story. I have taken refuge in the Lord, leaning not on my own understanding, refusing to blame God for my trouble, trusting that He has my back in whatever I face. Are some days harder than others? Absolutely. Have I had additional meltdowns? Absolutely. Has the thought come to me that I can't bear this? Absolutely. Have I desperately desired this cup to pass from me? Absolutely! Do I yet have joy in the midst of sorrow? Absolutely!

WHERE IS THE VICTORY?

My response to the question, "Where is the victory?" is that I am living in the victory right now. I am not waiting for the victory. I am experiencing the victory in a very real, tangible way. Sometimes we can be shortsighted as to believe that one final outcome reveals victory, but victory is displayed in many ways in real life.

Everything that has occurred in my life since March 13, 2015, I count as a victory for me and my family. Me graduating two months later was victory. Our children graduating from college was victory: Brendon (May 2016), Amber (May 2018), Emmanuel (December 2018), and Timothy from high school (May 2019). Timothy is now in his final year of college at Michigan State University. He will graduate with two degrees. The church is not only still standing but thriving. In my opinion—this is victory. My peace of mind is victory. Joy in serving the Lord is victory. Having a steadfast spirit to serve the Lord is victory. The determination to help people is victory.

Although it's not the script I would have written for my life, thus blindsided by this invasive entrance, we are going to roll with it. Let's see how God will turn this lemon into lemonade. There is nothing that I can do about what happened; therefore, I am focusing on our future that's ahead. As when a mother gives birth to a child there is pain, so is giving birth to dreams.

I feel like I must be carrying something that is significant, too significant to abort.

As I spoke with my daughter yesterday about her editing the book, she looked at me and said, "You always have fight in you. You can be knocked down in the boxing arena, and as the referee is doing the countdown, at nine you will lift your toe as an indication that you are not out." We laughed and went our way. I remember thinking that she knows me well, and her words actually encouraged me. I love that I am living that example before her. I want her to know that's her DNA as well.

Paul got so excited about the victory that he exclaimed in his writing, "Thanks be to God who giveth us the victory in our Lord Jesus Christ!" (1 Corinthians 15:57, KJV) "Amen, Paul!" as my husband would say. We already have the victory that was purchased for us by the death of our Lord and Savior, Jesus Christ.

The Apostle John described this victory as being of the nature that it overcomes the world:

For whatsoever is born of God overcometh the world: and this is the victory that overcometh the world, even our faith. Who is he that overcometh the world, but he that believeth that Jesus is the Son of God? —1 John 5:4-5 (KJV)

He is referring to this world's system that only comprises the lust of the flesh, the lust of the eyes, and the pride of life. In Christ, we have already been given everything we need to live a victorious life. We just need to believe.

NEVERTHELESS, NOT MY WILL

The moment had arrived in Jesus's journey where death was inevitable. He was in the Garden of Gethsemane, where He had often gone to spend time in prayer. This time, He had taken His inner-circle disciples: Peter, James, and John. He actually desired that they, too, would pray while He went further into the garden to speak with God.

On that occasion, Jesus actually asked the Father if the cup of death that He was about to taste could be removed from Him. Then He responded, "Nevertheless, not My will, but thine will be done" (Luke 22:43, KJV).

This prayer revealed the human side of Jesus—how He, being human, experienced what we experience. This is why He can be so in tune with our needs. He knew it was going to be nothing but pain ahead of Him as He was destined the next day to be crucified on a cross for the sins of the world. Who wants to know that kind of information ahead of time? He demonstrated, at all times, that He was here on earth to do the will of the Father.

God has a plan for us all. Many people try to run, hide, duck, and dodge the plan of God. People in their youth want to "experience life first." I have heard of young people referring to Christianity as something for "old folks." The enticement of the world, especially in our day, presents a tremendous hunger for what it appears to promise—health, wealth, success, relationships, esteem, and fame. Then, they look at what they perceive God requires and feel as if in some way the rewards don't compare. Or, they just ignore the idea of God altogether.

I decided long before I had met my husband that I had a "nevertheless" in me as well. The actual words I spoke to God in prayer were, "Lord, I will do whatever You want me to do." That is actually the only prayer that I remember, although I would get on my knees regularly to have conversations with God. Just as with my marital covenant, the script had already been written in terms of my commitment until the end; the same is true with my calling. I would never have dreamt of such a calling into ministry, but it fits my devotion to Christ so well.

Of course, truth be told, circumstances have always beat against my life, family, ministry, and finances daily in an attempt to make me to cry "uncle." I refuse to relent. Before the trial of my life, I would remind myself, from time to time, that there is no quit in me. Well, those words were tested under the most extreme heat. It felt like we had been thrown into a fiery furnace, like the three Hebrew boys in scripture. Yet, still, my resolve today as I write is, "Nevertheless, not my will but Your will be done."

THE JOURNEY CONTINUES....

I awakened today in great anticipation of finishing this chapter. Although the story isn't over, this book brings you up to date on where we are in the journey. Actually, I feel as though the writing of the book has been therapeutic for me. It has definitely been a vulnerable place to open up my life to the world. It is my hope that people can gain insight, inspiration, motivation, encouragement, empathy, courage, hope, and perseverance, amongst other virtues, to help in their life's journey.

I desire to see families be able to hear and heed the lessons shared, if they find themselves in similar circumstances. I am hoping that this can be a place of therapy and knitting of hearts for those who know and love us. In the words of my husband, "It is an honor to serve Him" (referring to Jesus). It

130 THE DAY *My Life Changed*

is also an honor to serve His people. For those whom we have served, thank you for the opportunity to leave an imprint in your lives. I have determined that for me, the only thing that's truly worthy of me devoting my entire life to is the gospel. This, I will never regret or feel ashamed of.

In my quest to read the Bible through in a year, today I happened to read about the Apostle Paul and his missionary journeys as he took the gospel to the world. I read about the sufferings that Jesus had spoken of during Paul's initiation into the kingdom, so to speak. He said, "He is a chosen vessel of Mine to bear My name before Gentiles, kings, and the children of Israel: For I will show him how many things he must suffer for My name's sake" (Acts 9:15-16, NKJV).

I have personally witnessed the price of the call in a variety of ways. Hindsight is always 20/20. Consider your own life. Are there things you would do differently if you knew differently? Of course there are. As it is said, "You live and you learn." I am the type who likes to learn my lesson the first time, if possible. Although I don't always accomplish that, it's my desire. Sometimes, it takes time to work truths into your life.

When everything is said and done, I have come to know God in ways and depths that I would never replace for a safe life of pleasure or an attempt to find an easier path to tread of lesser resistance. People who lead are people who have real lives, real struggles, real pain, and real families, just like everyone else. The opposition is just greater because of what they carry. My desire is for us all, God's team and family, to realize the ultimate destiny God has preplanned for us. And I request your continued prayers for us as the journey continues. . . .

My desire is for us all, God's team and family, to realize the ultimate destiny God has preplanned for us.

About the Author

Tanya has masterfully crafted this heartfelt book to encourage you in your storm—whether you're in one now, or it's on the way. She takes you on a real-life journey from her own tsunami that hit her family's life. As a certified life coach, Tanya takes the coaching approach to reveal strategies that aid when trauma has been experienced.

Being a three-time hall of fame athlete, she heavily leans on the champion within to help her overcome. Tanya is a speaker and practical leader who is clear about her passion: to help people build the life that they love, which her relentless no-quit attitude conveys.

Tanya earned her B.A. degree from Central Michigan University, double majoring in broadcasting and cinematic arts and journalism. She received her Master's degree in Theology from Moody Theological Seminary. Tanya is a native of Flint, Michigan, where she serves as a minister. She is wife of Pastor Timothy R. Stokes and mother of four children: Brendon, Amber, Emmanuel, and Timothy II.

OTHER BOOKS BY THE AUTHOR

Available directly from the author: *tanyacstokes@gmail.com*

Die Without Regrets (12 Ways to Unleash the Champion Inside You)

How I Lost 50 Pounds

101 Ways You Can Save Money

101 Ways You Can Save Money audiobook

Available at Amazon:

365 Days of Victory (Daily inspirational quotes to nurture the champion in you)

The Victory Journal (Writing smart goals)

Printed by BoD™in Norderstedt, Germany